The Leader's Guide to Quality in America

By

John Q. McMillian

©2008

Foreword

There is no substitute for excellence and there is no room for failure. John Q. McMillian was taught this philosophy by his parents and has lived by it throughout his years in the Air Force and private industry.

John's first real experience with organized quality training began in the early 1980's. As a launch crew commander, he maintained the highest possible standards for operational readiness with his crew and the Titan II Missile facility that was his responsibility. At that time, the military was just beginning to embrace the idea of service quality throughout its branches.

The Department of the Navy began in 1984 to improve organizational performance through the use of Total Quality Leadership (TQL) within its logistical organizations. Since that time, the practice of TQL has been implemented throughout the Navy and the rest of the armed forces.

The change from past "old school" management practices to TQL and a Lean Corporate Culture is substantial and impacts on the jobs of every person in America. Because of this, the transition to a Lean Culture and TQL must be planned for and put into place in a systematic fashion. The implementation process must be spearheaded by the organization's leader. Regardless of the size of the organization, any transformational effort must come from the top. A training program that provides all of the information necessary to get started with TQL and Lean Corporate Culture must be developed and made available to all employees of the organization. Participation in this training is not optional and every employee must adopt this philosophy. American business ceased being "price competitive" many years ago. The only way we can continue to maintain a differential advantage over the worldwide competition we now face is though achieving and maintaining the highest quality standards in the world for our products and services.

"Quality has to begin in the board room. It can never be better than what top management understands quality to be."
W. Edwards Deming

Purpose

This book provides an overview of the major elements of TQL and Lean Culture/Manufacturing, and it is a roadmap guiding a business leader in their implementation. *The Leader's Guide to Quality in America* includes the definition of TQL, underlying philosophy, implementation roles, management structure, and how the scientific method coupled; with Statistical Process Control and Lean Manufacturing concepts, are applied to improve work processes, eliminate waste, and reduce costs. While it is not a substitute for formal education and training, it provides solid information on the basics of the total quality approach and perhaps serves to dispel some misconceptions. This is a straight forward, no nonsense approach, to what it takes to internalize and adopt the quality philosophy and Lean Culture necessary to thrive in worldwide competition or to gain a competitive edge over the service business down the street from you!

Based on more than thirty years of a combination of military and industrial experience, there are certain conclusions that were easy to draw:

➢ The integrated application of quality management and Statistical Process Control (SPC) is feasible in a wide range of manufacturing and service organizations.

➢ Active participation of top leaders is a critical element for success. The program cannot be introduced as a ground up philosophy. All managers and supervisors must be fully trained and indoctrinated before the front line employees. All levels of management must be able to lead by example.

➢ Organizational changes must be made to establish and sustain improvement through the application of improved leadership skills, quality management, and SPC.

➢ The quality leadership approach suggested is based on the philosophy of W. Edwards Deming, the prominent quality consultant who contributed greatly to Japan's economic gains following WWII and heralded the beginning of the "new economic age" as he called it.

For additional information concerning TQL and the Deming approach, I recommend the following: *Deming Management at Work* by Mary Walton (1990) and *Thinking About Quality* by Lloyd Dobyns and Clare Crawford-Mason (1994). This book is based, in part, on the manual, *Total Quality Leadership: A Primer*, created by the Department of the Navy and I wish to thank them for their contributions.

Table of Contents

Chapter 1: Introduction

Total Quality Leadership, or TQL, provides the means for organizations, regardless of their size, to more efficiently and effectively respond to current and future trends in the world market place. I think we can all agree with W. Edwards Deming when he stated years ago that we were in a "new economic age". Gone is the age of mass production where the success of a business (or service) was based solely on the numbers of items produced or the amount of service provided. It is no longer sufficient to just talk about good quality or bad quality, we have got to be specific and we must include the needs and wants of the customer in any definition of quality we use.

What is Quality?

What does quality mean to you? How do you define quality? *What is more important how you define quality or how your customers define quality?*

From a manufacturing standpoint, we could talk conformance to specifications and tolerances. In a global sense, we might discuss the number of defects per hundred, or per thousand, or per million defect opportunities, as in what has become known as "Six Sigma Quality". But for now let's stick to the basics and just talk about conformance to requirements. In a nutshell, this simply means that we are going to build it like we say we are going to build it! We adhere to the specifications and tolerances that our product has been designed to meet.

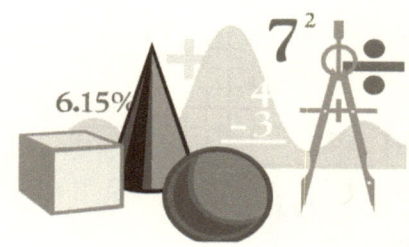

Conformance to requirements is absolutely fundamental! If we are unable to build a product (or deliver a service) like we say we are going to; then we are not even in the game of quality.

But is that enough?

Do you remember the Yugo? It was "the cutting edge of Serbo-Croatian automotive technology", at least according to comedian Dan Aykroyd in 1987. This car failed miserably in the American market place. It was only sold at retail for nine months; yet still today, one mention of it brings jokes and wisecracks from people who were not even born when it was first sold here! What happened? Certainly they built it as they said they would. The car conformed to all the requirements of the Yugo. *Yet still it failed!*

Conformance to requirements will get you in the game of quality; but it will not win the game for you! It's worth repeating, make no mistake – if you can't build it like you say you are going to build it, or deliver a service like you have promised, you will not even be in the game of quality!

Let's say we were going to manufacture ink pens. I am not talking about a high priced fancy pen, just your everyday ink pen. The design might look something like this:

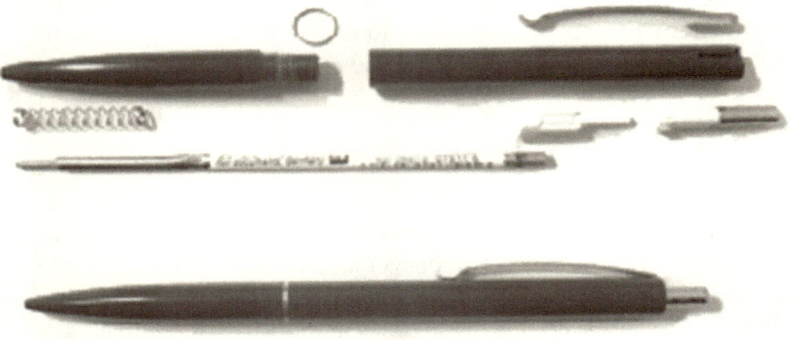

Based on our research, we would design the pen and create the specifications and tolerances. We would specify the color of the ink and how much goes in it. All the details would be established and we would begin to build the pens.

The real question is what does the consumer care about? The consumer rarely knows or even cares that the pen has a diameter of .375" +/- .001". All they care about it does it write! Does it do what it is supposed to do when they buy it and does it continue to do so for a reasonable period of time? That's what's often called fitness for use.

So, we might develop a definition of quality along the lines of: Quality is conformance to specifications and meeting or exceeding customer expectations and requirements - 100% of the time (for both our internal and external customers).

Quality Implications

Customer needs:

First, a company must have a complete understanding of their customer's needs. Ask the buyers what they are looking for in that particular product or service. Either conduct your own surveys or perhaps you can purchase surveys already conducted by marketing companies. Either way, this must be done – how else can you understand the needs of your customers? *You must talk to them!*

Product Specifications:

After the marketing department determines the customer's needs, the design people take over and develop the specifications necessary to meet those needs. This is where a lot of companies drop the ball. At this point they simply hand the designs to the manufacturing folks and say, "Ok, now it's your turn, go build it." They don't stop to ask the question, "Can you build this to our specifications?"

Process Design:

Companies must take into consideration if the manufacturing department can build the product (or can our crews deliver a service) to our specifications. The issue is, are the machines capable of building the product to those specifications and tolerances? I have seen this many times in industry. A company grows fast and develops a lot of products that the customers are delighted with (fitness for use), and yet in many cases, the products did not meet the design specifications and by definition (conformance to requirements) the company was building defects! Often, in this situation, product is needless scrapped or worse yet, people are told to go ahead and ship the "defective" product. These conflicting actions leave the front line employees confused and thinking that the company cares little for quality, *and sometimes, they are right.* When an organization finds itself in this situation, it must go back and evaluate each product. Does the design specification make sense as it relates to the needs of the customer and can manufacturing actually build it to specifications? Does it make sense for a company to have a specification to reject a fence post that is .125" to short, when the customer is going to put about two and a half feet of that post in the ground? Maybe, maybe not, it depends on the needs of the customer.

Raw Materials:

Every company must have the highest quality raw materials to use in the manufacturing process or in the services they provide. No matter how high the quality of the machines, or the operator's intentions, they can produce no higher quality than that of the raw materials. As the saying goes, "garbage in – garbage out"!

Monitor:

Everyone monitors the quality of the product or service they are responsible for. Everyone! No exceptions! For example, I rarely come into close contact with product in manufacturing plants. However, whenever I am on the floor, I am constantly observing forklifts and the crates they are moving – looking for signs of damage to the crates, which can indicate damage to the product within the crates.

Developing a 100% Philosophy

The 3M Corporation has a 100% Philosophy:

- A belief that every error has a cause(s) that can be identified and eliminated.
- An understanding that it's always cheaper to do it right the first time.
- A recognition that systems are a major source of errors.
- Planned and measurable movement over time toward the goal.

Managing Total Quality, 3M Corporation

The Cornerstones of TQL

TQL is an approach to quality management that is based upon six major elements or cornerstones. This section describes briefly those six cornerstones and presents information about some related concepts that are central to TQL:

1 **Definition.** TQL may be defined as the application of quantitative methods and the knowledge of people to assess and improve:

(a) materials and services supplied to the organization

(b) all significant processes within the organization

(c) meeting the needs of the end-user, now and in the future

This definition describes the "what" of TQL ("application of quantitative methods and the knowledge of people to assess and improve"), the "where" of the effort ("all significant processes [performed] within the organization") and the "when" ("now, and in the future"). "Significant" is used to emphasize that TQL practices should address processes *central* to business performance, not those that are incidental to it. This emphasis avoids committing scarce organizational resources to less important issues.

More about this definition of TQL in a few minutes!

2 **The Deming philosophy provides the basis for TQL.** W. Edwards Deming (1900-1993) was a physicist and statistician who developed a management philosophy for improving quality. The principal elements of the philosophy come from:

(a) theory of variation

(b) application of systems theory to managing organizations

(c) psychology of work

(d) use of the scientific method to pursue optimal corporate performance.

These elements were adapted for implementation in pre-World War ll American and post-War Japan, and subsequently in the rest of the world.

3 **Implementation approach.** The approach to implementation is two-phased (Doherty, 1990). The first phase concentrates on planning and conducting quality improvement efforts. Education and training resources for process improvement are required for success. The second phase advances and sustains the continual improvement throughout the organization, including suppliers. Strategic planning and management are used to enhance future organizational performance.

4 **Management structure.** Changes in systems and processes are managed through the organization's chain of command. Significant and critical processes typically cross functional areas. Therefore, cross-functional teams at the executive, middle, and supervisory levels must be linked for communication and coordination of efforts. These teams concentrate on gathering and applying information to improve effectiveness.

5 **A scientific approach.** The aim of TQL is to enhance organizational effectiveness. This can only be achieved by using an objective, disciplined approach to making changes in the processes and systems. The performance of current processes and systems is analyzed and an improvement plan is developed. This is called developing a Current State Map and then a Future State Map. The plan is carried out and performance is analyzed to determine the effects of changes. Changes that result in improvement are retained.

6 **Quality Council.** Finally, a Quality Council, composed of a cross-section of top management, supervisors, and front line employees is created to guide the organization's quality and Lean Manufacturing efforts.

Deming's 14 Points

A few years after World War II, the government of the United States sent W. Edwards Deming to Japan to help them reorganize and rebuild their devastated industries. He taught them a philosophy of leadership that allowed everyone to work together for the common good of the company. He gave them the profound knowledge necessary to compete in what he called the "new economic age". The Japanese attribute so much of their global success to Deming that they named their highest price for manufacturing quality after him! Even the very popular Toyota Production System (TPS) also know as Lean Manufacturing, has some of its roots in the Deming philosophy.

To achieve continued excellence in the new economic age, organizations must redirect their results-oriented management practices into a process-oriented way of thinking. Looking at the process allows each of us to make small, but continuous improvements in how we do our jobs.

Here is Deming's leadership philosophy boiled down and condensed into what he simply called, "The 14 Points".

1   Create constancy of purpose toward improvement of product and service, with the aim to become competitive and to stay in business, and to provide jobs.

2   Adopt the new philosophy. We are in a new economic age. Western management must awaken to the challenge, must learn their responsibilities, and take on leadership for change.

3   Cease dependence on inspection to achieve quality. Eliminate the need for inspection on a mass basis by building quality into the product in the first place.

4   End the practice of awarding business on the basis of price tag. Instead, minimize total cost. Move toward a single supplier for any one item, on a long-term relationship of loyalty and trust.

5   Improve constantly and forever the system of production and service, to improve quality and productivity, and thus constantly decrease costs.

6   Institute training on the job.

7   Institute leadership. The aim of supervision should be to help people and machines and gadgets to do a better job. Supervision of management is in need of overhaul, as well as supervision of production workers.

8   Drive out fear, so that everyone may work effectively for the company.

9 Break down barriers between departments. People in research, design, sales, and production must work together as a team, to foresee problems of production and in use that may be encountered with the product or service.

10 Eliminate slogans, exhortations, and targets for the work force asking for zero defects and new levels of productivity. Such exhortations only create adversarial relationships, as the bulk of the causes of low quality and low productivity belong to the system and thus lie beyond the power of the work force.

11 a. Eliminate work standards (quotas) on the factory floor. Substitute leadership. b. Eliminate management by objective. Eliminate management by numbers, numerical goals. Substitute leadership.

12 a. Remove barriers that rob the hourly worker of his right to pride of workmanship. The responsibility of supervisors must be changed from sheer numbers to quality. b. Remove barriers that rob people in management and in engineering of their right to pride of workmanship. This means, *inter alia*, abolishment of the annual or merit rating and of management by objective.

13 Institute a vigorous program of education and self-improvement.

14 Put everybody in the company to work to accomplish the transformation. The transformation is everybody's job.

(Walton, 1990)

Basic Concepts

In addition to the six cornerstones of TQL, other important concepts are:

Internal customers and end-users

The term "customers" refers to those people who buy and/or use products and services. In the world of commerce, customers ultimately define quality. Under TQL, the focus of quality improvement efforts is to meet our organizational goals and objectives. The "customer" is not only the end user. All organizations have internal customers as well. The internal customer is simply the next step in the process.

Quality focus

This has to include both our internal and our external customers. No matter the customer, our goal is to make sure they are not just satisfied, but absolutely delighted with our product and/or services.

Continuous improvement

All organizational must continue to improve and grow otherwise, more dynamic companies with devour their market share. There is a simple phrase that summarizes this idea, *innovate or die!*

"The price of success is perseverance. The price of failure comes cheaper."

Anonymous

Chapter 2:
Back to the Basics

Process improvement

Process improvement involves systematically analyzing and changing process factors so that they work together better to improve both process quality and efficiency. Organizational effectiveness is increased through improvement, redesign, or innovation of processes. Processes are improved when they are more predictable, more efficient, cost less, and contribute more to meeting task requirements. Through process improvement efforts, problems and/or errors are prevented rather than fixed after they have occurred.

This is not the traditional "Suggestion Box" approach to improvements. If you have a suggestion box hanging on the wall, get rid of it! No one is using it and rarely are the suggestions even being read or given credit where credit is due when they are used. This is a true, organization wide, process improvement effort, under the direction of the Quality Council. It is an adaptation of Deming's Point 5 and is often called Kaizen. Kaizen efforts are focused on the process, rather than achieving a specific result (as is often the case in traditional American companies). As originally conceived, Kaizen was a slow, ongoing process with involvement from everyone in the organization – management and front line employees alike. Of course, with our need for speed and haste in doing things, we have Americanized the concept to include things like "Kaizen Events" where intense efforts for process improvement are directed to one specific process. This personally does not appeal to me. For me, it misses the true mark of the organizational wide improvements and often gives the people involved in the "event" very little training in the background, techniques, and philosophy of process improvements.

Process management

Process management involves the leadership actions required to begin and sustain continuous improvement of significant processes. This is the primary role of the Quality Council. The Quality Council acts as the rudder on the ship of quality.

Extended process

An organization must work with customers and suppliers as part of an extended system to improve quality. Customers can provide information that helps an organization to focus its improvement efforts on those product and service characteristics that have the greatest impact on quality. Suppliers provide products or services that affect an organization's ability to achieve its goals. Working with suppliers to clarify current needs or to share process improvements can reduce problems and avoid defects due to faulty materials or inadequate service.

Definition of Total Quality Leadership

Our definition of TQL (page 10) is based on Deming's flow diagram that shows production as a system (Deming, 1986) (See Figure 3, page 24 of this document). Now let's take a closer at the implications of this definition of total quality leadership.

"The application of quantitative methods . . ."

The term "quantitative methods" refers to statistical and other graphical tools that summarize data in a structured way (Brassard & Ritter, 1994). These methods help in the identification, understanding and control of factors related to acceptable or poor performance. (See Chapter 10, page 77)

". . . and the knowledge of people . . ."

Most process information does not reside in the existing financial accounting or management information systems. Rather, process information is in the minds of the people — front line employees, team leaders, supervisors, and managers who are responsible for a process. It's not just individual knowledge that is important, but the collective knowledge of all those who are involved with the process. People in the process must work *as a team* to contribute to the information, ideas, and actions needed to improve a process. One of the principal differences between TQL and some traditional problem-solving approaches (e.g., task forces, special purpose teams, focus groups) is that the people doing the analysis and improvement are *process owners*, i.e., those who are already responsible for process performance. As indicated during the discussion of the "extended process" concept, the knowledge of customers and suppliers is also very valuable in understanding and improving processes.

". . . to assess and improve . . ."

TQL uses measurement and statistical analysis to (1) assess the causes of process problems and (2) evaluate the effects of changes to the system. The scientific approach to process improvement requires that process performance be assessed and understood *prior* to making changes to it. Improvement of a process involves changing factors that strongly influence or "cause" process performance. These factors are often grouped into four categories: materials, methods, people, and machines. (See Cause and Effect Diagrams, page 62, for additional information.) The most significant factors require action by management to achieve lasting gains in improvement. For example, improving the performance of a supply center's process might involve changing the delivery times of supplies from a contractor, changing employee training, or revising work procedures. An individual or work group probably would not have the authority to make these changes. This is one of the fundamental reasons for the Quality Council to work on a process. Assessment and improvement of all essential processes are fundamental to TQL. When processes are assessed initially there may be a lot of waste and redundancy in process steps. Teams are able to identify and eliminate waste, which will lower costs almost immediately. This reduction in costs can then be invested in innovations to that particular process or to other processes. This reinvestment strategy can only be leadership-directed: the decisions concerning what to do with the cost savings are ones that must be based upon management priorities.

". . . all significant processes within the organization . . ."

Significant processes are directly related to the company's performance. They are the activities that produce the products or services of an organization. These processes are aided by internal operations that are necessary, but by themselves do not meet the overall goals of an organization. For example, providing meals, offering technical training, and maintaining employee records might contribute indirectly to a company's performance. This highlights the fact that everyone in an organization contributes to the overall quality of the product or service produced by the company. Even the janitors that clean up the bathrooms at night contribute to the quality of the company products or services. Improving these processes may be a secondary priority; however, they are a priority none the less.

". . . now, and in the future."

"Now" means improving quality of current processes. The "future" refers to preparing for evolving or anticipated organizational changes. TQL embraces both present and future through the two-phase implementation approach. The first phase focuses on continuous improvement of existing processes that are responsible for current effectiveness. The second phase includes re-engineering processes or creating new products and services to meet the anticipated needs of end-users — internal and external customers.

"Each problem has hidden in it an opportunity so powerful that it literally dwarfs the problem. The greatest success stories were created by people who recognized a problem and turned it into an opportunity."

Joseph Sugarman

Chapter 3: Applications

Adoption of the Deming Philosophy

The leadership of progressive organizations initially adopt the Deming approach because (1) productivity needed to increase to respond to potential competition, (2) the leaders recognized the approach could address those management practices in their community that inhibited productivity (Dockstader, 1984), and (3) because of its proven effectiveness both in Japan and the United States.

The Economic Rationale for the Practice of TQL

The economic rationale that underlies the Deming philosophy is the chain reaction of quality and productivity. Deming proposed that improved quality leads to improved productivity which, in turn, leads to business survival and growth (1986).

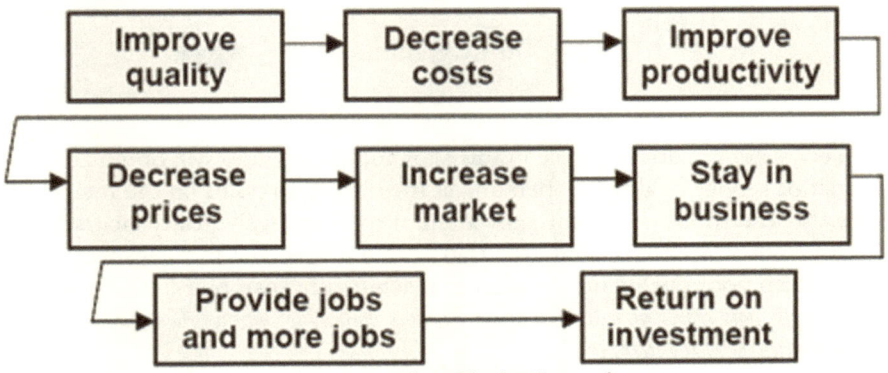

Figure 1 The Chain Reaction

Understanding the relationship between improved quality and decreased costs depends upon different assumptions and approaches to productivity. In the past, most people equated improved quality with increased inspection and, therefore, believed that improving quality increased costs and lowered productivity. Under TQL the assumption is that if the causes of poor quality are prevented in the first place, there is a reduction in inspection and rework costs. These savings alone should lead to productivity improvement. It is important to understand the difference between these two ways of achieving quality.

Quality by inspection

When enhanced performance is pursued through inspection, improvement is based upon failure. The focus of management is on producing products or services, then sorting the good from the bad. Improvement efforts under this approach tend to concentrate on increasing throughput or reducing production costs. Quality is managed by finding defects and errors through inspections and audits. Costs of this approach include the cost of performing the work the first time, the costs of inspection, and the costs of recovering from failures.

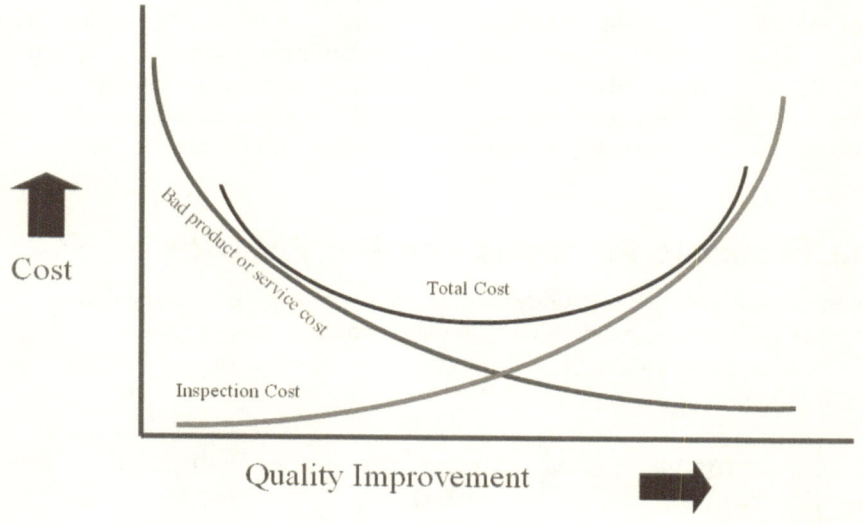

Since costs are the driving force in this situation, companies will optimize product or service quality by operating at the minimum point on the total cost curve. With efforts such as this, any attempt to "improve" quality incurs increased costs. Improvement efforts are often just adding more inspectors (to try and keep poor quality products from reaching the customer). *This type of improvement effort drives up costs and worse yet, does nothing to improve the process that created the defects in the first place!*

"You cannot inspect quality into the product; it is already there. 100% inspection will guarantee trouble."

W. Edwards Deming

Quality by prevention

The prevention approach to quality improvement is based upon the assumption that high or low quality is an outcome of the process that is used to produce the product or service. If the process — the interaction of people, machines, methods, and materials works well, then high quality will result. Walter Shewhart, a statistician and contemporary of Deming, confirmed this assumption at the Bell Telephone Laboratories (Shewhart, 1939). Use of this approach deters failures, the costs of failure, and the reliance on inspections.

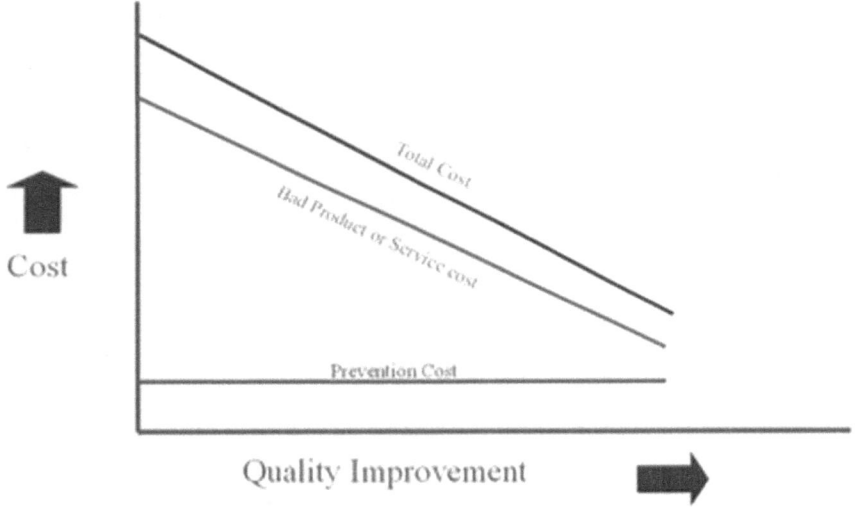

However, there are several reasons why the inspection approach continues to be the dominant approach to quality:

1. Some inspections must be conducted to avoid threats to life and property.

2. People do not clearly understand the important differences between inspection and prevention approaches to quality.

3. People do not think they are able to make changes that could prevent failures.

4. Changing to a new system involves risk taking, and the fear of failure leads to conservative decisions (Suarez, 1993).

5. It is frequently easier and more rewarding to respond to the urgency of a failure than to take the actions required to avoid problems.

The Three Components of the Deming Philosophy

Deming's quality philosophy is based on profound knowledge, leadership principles, and the learning cycle. The system of profound knowledge leads to the practice of those principles that, in turn, lead to the use of the learning cycle (also known as the continuous improvement cycle or the "Plan-Do-Check-Act [PDCA]" cycle). Using the learning cycle can increase profound knowledge. Descriptions of the three components follow.

System of Profound knowledge

Profound knowledge provides the knowledge and theory needed to understand and improve organizations. It is made up of four interrelated parts: (1) *theory of knowledge* (the development, testing, and application of hypotheses), (2) *theory of variation* (identifying factors and interactions that affect quality through measurement and analysis of data), (3) *general systems theory* (understanding and dealing with the dynamics of internal organizational components and the interrelationships of an organization with its external environment), and *(4) psychology in the workplace* (finding and using effective teaching, communication, incentives, and teamwork skills). Deming indicates that one need not be an expert in any one of these areas, but rather have a working knowledge of all four areas to make improvements.

Deming's "14 Points" of leadership

Deming describes 14 leadership principles (page 12) that are derived from profound knowledge. They are also known as obligations because leaders are seen as being directly responsible for their adoption and incorporation into an organization. The aim of the 14 Points is to improve performance while eliminating harmful beliefs and practices. Deming believed that the 14 Points describe a management *system* that cannot be applied on a piecemeal basis. All are required to ensure the future success of organizations.

Application of the scientific method

The "PDCA" cycle (Figure 2) will be presented in greater detail at a later time. It can be described as the systematic study of the causes of variation in quality and an approach to improving quality. The PDCA cycle involved the following steps:

1. Plan a change for improvement

2. Carry out the change on a small scale

3. Analyze and interpret effects of the change

4. Act on what was learned

5. Repeat step 1, with new knowledge

6. Repeat step 2, and onward.

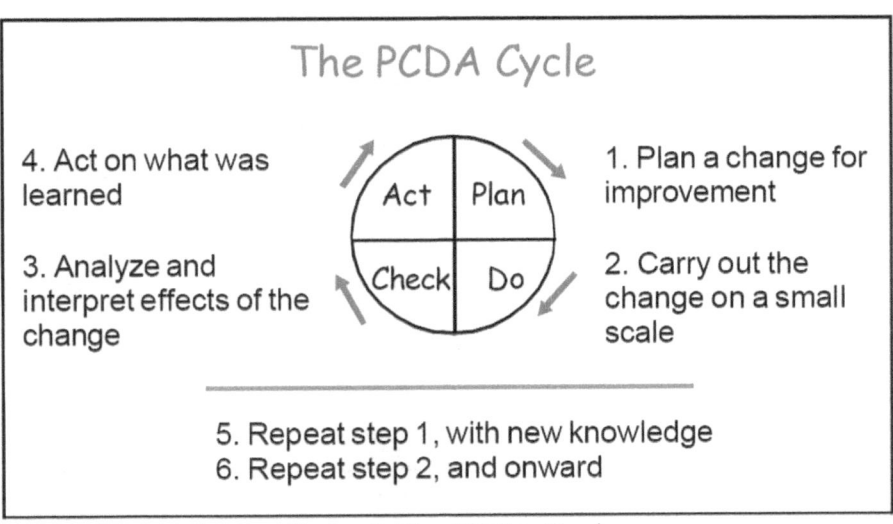

The PCDA Cycle

4. Act on what was learned

Act | Plan

Check | Do

3. Analyze and interpret effects of the change

1. Plan a change for improvement

2. Carry out the change on a small scale

5. Repeat step 1, with new knowledge
6. Repeat step 2, and onward

Figure 2 The PDCA Cycle

A benefit of using the cycle is increased knowledge to understand, predict, and control output. Because this application of the scientific method is cyclical and ongoing, and because the components of profound knowledge interact, the growth in knowledge is much like compounding interest — multiplicative rather than additive.

Viewing and Managing Organizations as Systems

A fundamental premise of Deming's theory of quality management is that an organization behaves as a system. Organizational effectiveness is greatest when the parts of that system work well together to achieve an aim or goal. Such a system is then optimized. Deming depicted this premise in a diagram (Figure 3). There are several very important implications from viewing an organization as a system.

System optimization requires that an organization is led and managed to focus on the aim of the organization. In Deming's diagram, the consumer research is the starting place, which begins with assessing consumer satisfaction with current products and services.

The systems perspective includes customers and suppliers. An external customer orientation is necessary to provide an aim for an organization.

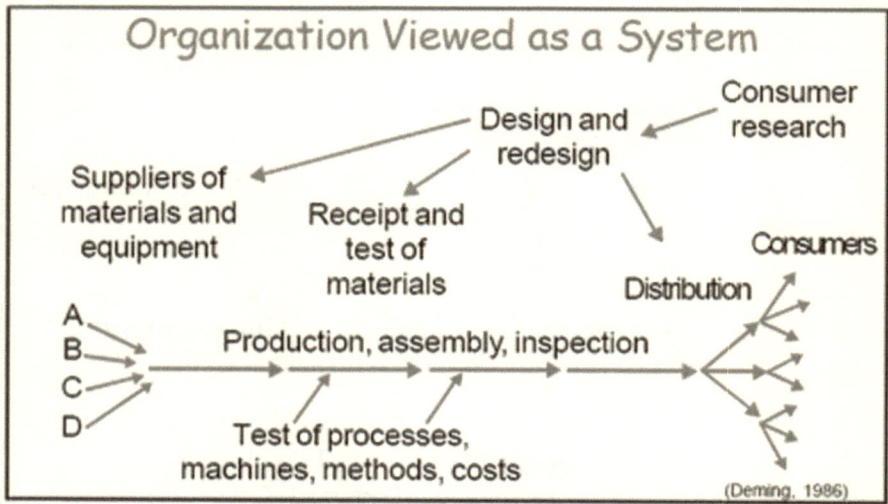

Figure 3 The Organization View as a System

Without an aim, the organization's activities can become scattered or internally focused. Figure 3 shows that consumer information is used to design the production or service process. Tests are performed and changes made to the process to satisfy the requirements revealed from the consumer research. As compelling as the argument is for focusing an organization on what is requested by customers, there may be beliefs and practices of an organization that make it difficult to use this approach. Examples are:

➢ A hierarchical perspective that can encourage members of functional departments to be self-serving and more responsive to departmental goals than to organizational ones.

➢ Performance appraisal and reward systems that can concentrate on individual behavior and subsequently reinforce efforts based on self-interest rather than the long term interests and performance requirements of the organization.

➢ Lack of constancy of purpose or aim, which can cause fragmented, unfocused work efforts.

➢ Emphasis on short-term gains and short-term thinking, which doesn't permit focus on strategic goals.

➢ Hope for easy, simple, and quick solutions to major problems that require little or no leader involvement.

➢ The belief that just solving problems, automating processes, or installing new equipment will result in optimum performance without considering the whole system. Actions based on this belief can lead to increased work complexity and degraded performance.

➤ Reliance on a quality control department to take care of performance problems. Deming labeled these beliefs and practices "deadly and dreadful diseases" of management. Holding these beliefs will not lead to overall sustained organizational improvement. Deming's "14 Points" are practices that seek to ameliorate the "deadly and dreadful diseases" while promoting a long-term commitment to optimizing organizational performance.

For further information and discussion of these points, a bibliography is provided. A good starting point is *The Deming Route to Quality and Productivity* by William W. Scherkenbach (1988).

The Role of Leaders

The leaders of an organization have the prime responsibility for the quality produced by the organization. The commitment and participation of leaders have long been recognized as critical factors in successful organizations (Tichy & Devanna, 1990). Only leaders have the sufficient authority, influence, and access to information to begin and maintain major organizational change. In support of these leadership practices, Deming identified some responsibilities and characteristics unique to leaders (Suarez, 1992). It is the responsibility of leaders to:

➤ Teach their people how the work of the group supports the aims of the organization.

➤ Act as a coach and counselor, rather than simply as a judge.

➤ Not rely solely on formal authority, rather develop systems knowledge and interpersonal skills.

➤ Be an unceasing learner. Encourage everyone to study.

➤ Create an environment that encourages participation and innovation.

"Opportunities? They are all around us...there is power lying latent everywhere waiting for the observant eye to discover it."
Orison Swett Marden

Chapter 4: Implementation

Approach

TQL is best implemented in two phases. The first phase concentrates on conducting quality improvement and Lean Culture training and establishing the resources needed to maintain the practice of TQL. Process management is the means to accomplish this phase. The second phase involves extending process management to all significant processes important to the goals of the organization, working with suppliers and end-users, and meeting the needs of the end user in the future. Strategic management is the means to accomplish this second phase.

The two-phase approach takes into account organizational realities. This phased approach was designed because:

1. Organizations do not have the resources to improve the entire organization at once.

Phase One provides an approach for deciding what to work on first and how to apply new methods for improvement.

2. Education and training need to be coupled with improvement initiatives so that they are provided at the appropriate time. A sequential company-wide training plan is part of the implementation plan developed by senior leaders during this phase.

3. The commitment of senior leaders to improvement efforts and the cultural transformation are absolutely critical at Phase One. Senior leaders must provide unwavering support for the program initiatives, regardless of their innermost personal feelings. Less that 100% commitment will encourage dissention among the mid-level managers and subsequently the front line employees.

4. Lessons learned from a company's quality improvement initiatives need to be understood and impediments to process management removed before expanding the application of TQL. Phase Two provides an approach to exploit this learning.

Process Management

Phase One establishes the practice of process management. The major steps of process management are (1) identification and training of employees to undertake initial improvement projects, (2) undertaking initial projects to gain experience with and obtain results from process management, (3) expansion and support of efforts to improve significant processes, and (4) removal of organizational impediments to improvement. This approach, depicted in Figure 4, can be applied to any organization.

Senior Leader Responsibilities for Leading Process Management	Improve	Educate & train	•Educate/train senior leader and executive-level group •Select/train support personnel •Train quality improvement teams
	Mission	Initiate project efforts	•Develop TQL implementation plan •Create a quality environment •Provide resources •Charter quality improvement teams •Establish the practice of commandwide process management
	Performance	Support/ extend process management efforts	•Plan for the reinvestment of resources •Identify/remove impediments •Monitor/assess progress •Act on teams' recommendations •Extend education/process management efforts

Figure 4 Senior Leader Responsibilities for Process Management

Process management differs from traditional operations management in a number of ways. It is:

1. *Proactive management* that seeks to identify and remove causes of errors to prevent occurrences of failures. Traditional management of quality tends to deal with failures after the fact through problem-solving.

2. *A team effort* that seeks to involve as team members all those responsible for and involved in the process.

3. *Based on objective sources of measurement to support decisions,* using data, statistical methods and decision rules for taking actions on processes. Measurement sources include *input* (materials from suppliers), the *output* (products and services) provided by an organization, and the *processes* (interaction of people, materials, methods, and machines) that produce the products and services.

4. *Continuous,* an ongoing pursuit of improvement, rather than episodic or crisis-driven. Leaders will still respond to problems, but they will focus on *prevention* of

problems through continuous improvement of the processes that lead to corporate effectiveness.

To practice TQL, the leader must establish process management as the day-today management methodology. An organizational unit (strategic business unit) is the focus for implementation of process management.

The knowledge and skills required for process management include systems thinking, team leadership, applied statistics, and the psychology of work. As a cost-effective training approach, leaders should send key employees to TQL courses to become trainers within their own organizations.

Strategic Management

The second phase of implementation extends continuous improvement and the Lean Culture to the strategic level, focusing on system wide implementation and alignment of work processes and management support systems. Phase Two implementation addresses the issues of (1) sustaining improvement efforts when leadership changes, (2) removing organizational structure and bureaucracy that inhibit change, and (3) identifying and meeting future corporate requirements or needs of end-users.

The methodology for guiding changes during Phase Two is strategic planning and strategic management. Specific guidance for strategic planning is presented in *A Handbook for Strategic Planning* by Wells and Doherty (1994); guidance for strategic management is given in *Strategic Management for Senior Leaders: A Handbook for Implementation* by Wells (1996).

Strategic planning is defined as "the process by which the guiding members of an organization envision its future and develop the necessary procedures and operations to achieve that future" (adapted from Goodstein, Nolan, & Pfeiffer, 1992). Strategic management is then the "management system that links strategic planning and decision-making with the day-today business of operations management" (Gluck, Kaufman, & Walleck, 1982). (See Figure 5) The strategic approach is a top-down systematic way to institutionalize what the organization does and how it accomplishes its goals. It focuses on current and future processes, integrating overall goals, and helps leaders understand the implications of aligning management systems so that they are all focused on the corporation, the customer, and the future. Strategic management requires the same tools and management approaches used during Phase One, with a greater emphasis on systems thinking and measurement.

While process management primarily focuses on improving current processes, strategic management focuses on ensuring the organization is working on the "right" processes to meet current and future requirements. The strategic approach is a systems method for changing the overall organization, not a process-by-process approach as used when getting started in process management.

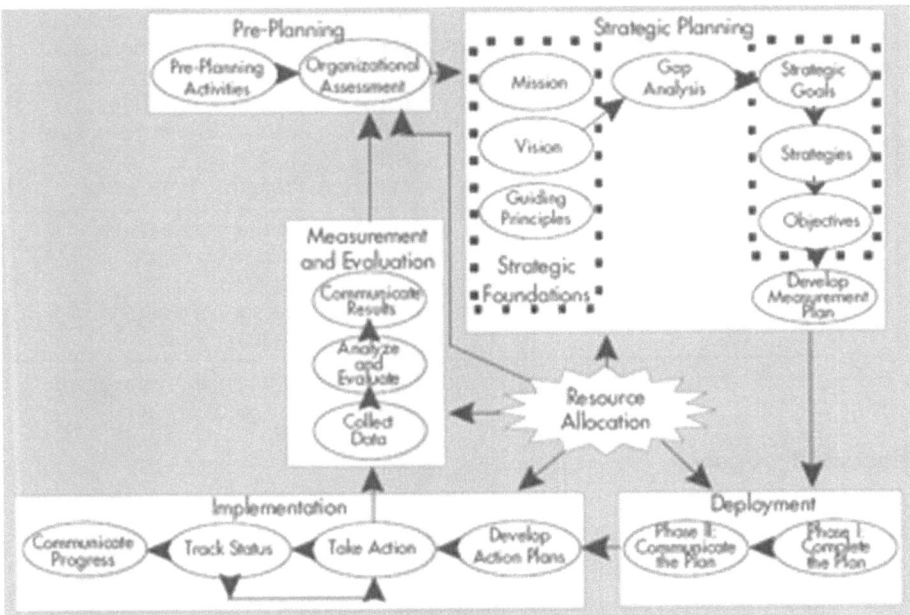

Figure 5 Strategic Management Model

The senior leaders are responsible for managing system wide changes necessary to optimize corporate effectiveness. They must develop and implement the strategic plan, committing the time, guidance, and resources necessary to achieve success. Some of the major leader activities in strategic planning and management are expanded on in Figure 6.

Strategic planning

The leaders set the aim and direction for the organization by clarifying (1) the *mission* — why the organization exists, whom it serves and what it provides, (2) the *vision* — a view of the organization that addresses needs of the end-users in the future, and (3) *guiding principles* — a reflection of the values of the organization, the quality philosophy, and how these values are to be employed in day-to-day management and decision-making. Organizational goals are then developed to reflect what needs to be done to move toward the vision. *Strategies* are the operational statements that describe how the strategic goals are going to be achieved. *Objectives* are the specific, measurable short-term and mid-term performance targets that represent interim steps for achieving the strategies.

Senior Leader Responsibilities for Leading Strategic Management	Improve Mission Effectiveness	Strategic Planning	• Set the aim and direction for organization • Develop goals & strategies to meet needs of future • Provide resource & support for implementation
		Deployment & Implementation Plans	• Develop plan of action for implementation • Communicate plan throughout organization • Use cross-functional teams working on goals
		Strategic Measures	• Develop mission effectiveness measures • Link effectiveness measures to input/process/ output measures • Assess progress on goals/make decisions
		Management Policies/ Support Studies	• Identify & change policies to match goals • Align organizational structure to match organizational aim & direction • Change accounting & personnel systems to map to organizational requirements

Figure 6 Senior Leader Responsibilities for Strategic Management

Execution of plans

Everyone in the organization will participate in strategic management, beginning with the leaders. Senior leaders begin by reaching consensus on goals and developing a plan of action. They then obtain input from their immediate subordinates, or direct reports, prior to publication. The plan is then communicated widely, with actions identified that are needed to achieve the goals and objectives. Leaders need to ensure that plans contain measurable milestones so that progress can be tracked.

Implementation

By turning the strategic plan into action, the organization aligns its significant work processes and identifies other management systems that need to be changed. While planning is top-down, implementation begins at the level where specific objectives are worked on, leading to accomplishment of strategies and, ultimately, goals. Roles and responsibilities for meeting goals are defined. Organizations with a well-established cross-functional team structure should use it where possible since organizational goals more than likely will be cross-functional. For goals defining new tasks, additional teams may need to be established. Through this infrastructure, plans for day-today business are linked and resource needs identified.

Strategic Measurement

Measures that indicate task effectiveness (outcome measures) will be developed. These should reflect how well strategic initiatives (i.e., goals to move toward the vision) are being met. Most current performance measures focus on efficiency or financial measures (e.g., amount of funds expended at end of the fiscal year). While these may be necessary for day-to-day business management and may be useful for investigating why an organization is not accomplishing its strategic goals, they may not be measuring task effectiveness or how well end-user needs are being met. Nor do these types of goals measure customer satisfaction.

Strategic Management and PDCA

The leadership uses the PDCA cycle to revise the strategic management effort. Organizational improvements are strategically "Planned." The planned changes are then deployed and implemented, reflecting the "Do" phase. Progress on objectives and goals is "Checked" and "Acted" upon, using the appropriate performance measures. Actions based on this information can include developing new plans to continue the cycle of improvement.

Organizational Implications of Strategic Management

As quality improvement activities become strategically oriented and widespread in an organization under Phase Two, there will be effects on all organizational systems. As an organization matures in its application of TQL:

➤ There will be shorter chains of command and fewer functional structures because cross-functional teams will be managing the work processes.

➤ Decision-making will shift lower in the organization because teams will control work processes.

➤ Information and reporting requirements will change to support cross-functional work on organizational goals.

➤ Organizational structure will evolve to a customer-focused or process-oriented structure.

➤ Compensation and reward systems will need to become more clearly aligned with performance and organizational goals.

These issues and others should be addressed when the strategic plan is revised. By using the strategic management process for directing organizational change, an organization's components will become aligned and integrated to maximize overall performance.

In summary, strategic planning and management are intended to help organizational components work together with a common purpose toward a shared vision. They are a way of aligning all work processes and involving customers and suppliers to help determine and meet future requirements. Strategic planning and management can be used to gain support from a parent company for the course charted by the plan and to obtain needed resources external to the organization. The plan and management efforts demonstrate the organization's commitment to providing quality products and services, both now, and in the future.

"The greatest waste in America is failure to use the abilities of people."

W. Edwards Deming

Chapter 5:
Roles & Structure

TQL Roles and Management Structure

At the beginning of TQL implementation, participation must be planned and *managed from the top* for two basic reasons: (1) the training needed to get underway is substantial and requires resource decisions, and (2) the selection of initial processes for improvement requires decision-making at the highest level to ensure buy-in and success.

Process Management and the Structure of Teams

Teams need to be formed that reflect existing ownership responsibilities and the way the work is actually performed. Contrary to the way management structures appear on hierarchical organization charts, work is actually accomplished through processes that flow horizontally, *across* the organization. The up-and-down vertical flow on the current organizational charts only reflects how control is exerted from the top to the bottom, an effective structure for communication top-down. However, "vertical" is not how the work flows, which is why the hierarchical structure may be a barrier to efficient processes (Rummler & Brache, 1991).

Organizations that focus on hierarchical relationships can suffer from competition and rivalries between functional areas, poor communications, and narrow perceptions of managerial responsibilities. Avoiding these barriers to performance and promoting the effective use of teams require knowledgeable leadership attention.

An important task of management is to span functional boundaries so that the output from one functional area meets the needs of the functional area receiving the product (the internal customer). At each step, value is added so that what is produced is a value added output for the external customer.

TQL teams

In an organization practicing TQL, teams are created to represent the top, middle, and working levels of an organization. The highest-level team is called an Executive Steering Committee (ESC) also often referred to as the company's Quality Council. Teams of mid-level leaders are called Quality Management Boards (QMBs). Teams of individuals who, work in a process, are called Process Action Teams (PATs) or Associate Involvement Teams (AITs). While all three levels of teams are expected to share a common approach to improvement, the PDCA cycle, they have different roles and responsibilities, as shown in Figure 7.

Quality Council/ESC

The Quality Council/ESC collects and uses information from the organization's customers and other external groups (e.g., regulatory agencies). It develops an implementation plan and selects improvement goals. It charters and supports the analysis and improvement efforts conducted by subordinate teams. It provides guidance to the Kaizen improvement efforts. The teams make recommendations to the Quality Council. During Phase Two the Quality Council/ESC is responsible for strategic planning and strategic management, implementing the management changes needed to optimize corporate effectiveness.

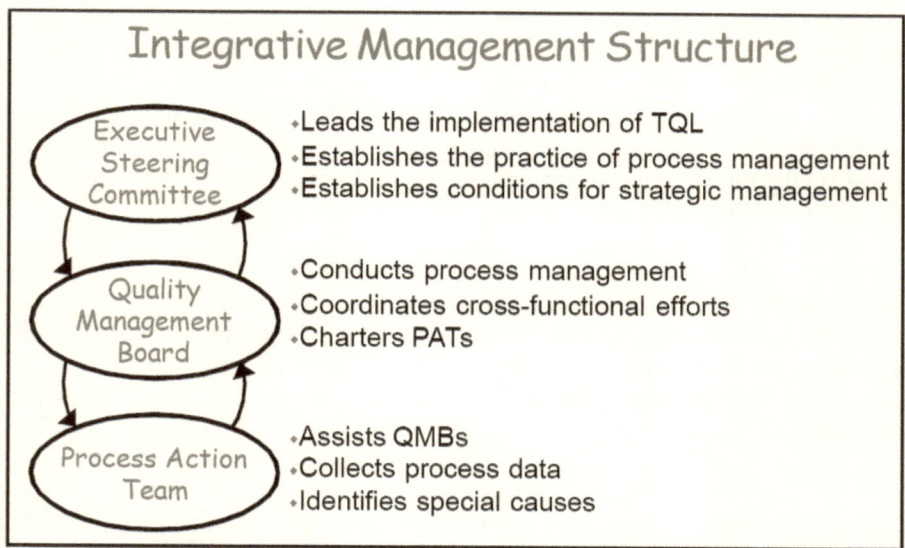

Figure 7 Integrative Management Structure

QMBs

QMBs are cross-functional teams of top and mid-level managers chartered by the ESC who are jointly responsible for significant processes. A QMB uses the combined knowledge of its members to select the process areas or factors that contribute the most toward achieving performance improvement. As needed, QMBs organize subordinate teams, PATs, to collect and analyze information to identify the process factors influence the quality of performance. Using the process data, QMBs make changes by removing impediments or changing the process. If QMBs identify changes that require a higher level of authority, then they submit those recommended changes to the ESC for action.

PATs

PATs (Process Action Teams or Associate Involvement Teams) are made up of front line employees who work directly in a process. These teams are chartered by a QMB to assist in the process management effort because of their (1) knowledge of process performance and (2) location in the process where data are to be collected. A critical responsibility of PATs is to collect, analyze, and provide summary information to QMBs about processes. PATs also take actions to stabilize process performance. If they identify changes that they cannot make at their level of authority, then they submit those changes as recommendations through the chain of command to QMBs.

The TQL teams are supported by internal consultants known as TQL coordinators and quality advisors. A TQL coordinator is the individual selected to support the ESC, while quality advisors support QMBs and PATs. TQL coordinators and quality advisors provide just-in-time training and assistance in the application of management and planning methods, process analysis tools, and principles of effective teamwork. These people are trained to provide this assistance through completion of TQL courses and past experience in the area of quality management and Lean Manufacturing concepts.

TQL Team Structure and
the Organization's Chain of Command

Quality improvement is managed through this team structure to provide an efficient means to optimize the performance of the organization. The organization's chain of command is responsible for improving work and management systems. For most companies with several hierarchy levels, it is likely that process improvement and management will involve two or more levels in the organization. Linking the teams, from higher to lower levels, is accomplished through an individual from a higher-level team who serves as a "linking pin." The linking pin is responsible for clarifying the subordinate team's charter to avoid an overlap or omission of improvement activities. Both the team structure and the use of linking pins are intended to maintain an effective chain of command and ensure focused improvement efforts.

In summary, effective process management requires organizing people who are process owners into teams. Given the focus on corporate performance, the application of TQL should not be viewed as a voluntary initiative for managers, supervisors, and team leaders. *At any level of leadership in an organization, participation in this program is not voluntary and they must provide unconditional support to the program, regardless of their innermost feelings!* "Bad mouthing" the program is grounds for disciplinary action at this level of the organization! Everyone in an organization is expected to contribute to the company's overall effectiveness and should be part of applying TQL tools and methods. They must be taught how to perform as effective team members or team leaders and how to apply the scientific approach to the improve processes. Having said that, if after training, a front line associate does not wish to volunteer to be on a team, *do not force them to join!* The company is better off having teams made up of people that want to participate, rather than having people on teams that will gripe and cause trouble. *One bad apple will spoil the whole bunch!*

While participation and the use of teams are important aspects of TQL, they do not eliminate the authority and responsibility of senior leaders to make unilateral decisions as required.

"Opportunity rarely knocks on your door. Knock rather on opportunity's door if you ardently wish to enter."
B.C. Forbes

Chapter 6:
The Scientific
Method

Application of the Scientific Method

Application of the scientific method to organizational performance is conducted through the "Plan-Do-Check-Act" (PDCA) cycle. The PDCA cycle is an objective method of acquiring and applying knowledge to improve performance. This cycle was developed and applied by Walter Shewhart (1939) as a way to improve the production systems of organizations. Figure 2, displayed earlier in this book, is Deming's version of this cycle (Deming, 1986).

Use of the PDCA Cycle

Figure 2 (page 23) shows a procedure for improving quality by making process changes. The types of changes that are evaluated could be (1) actions taken to avoid deterioration of the current performance due to unexpected events, such as accidents or emergencies, or (2) those designed to improve future performance of a process or system. In both of these circumstances, a "Plan" needs to be formulated, "Do" is the execution of that plan, and "Check" is an evaluation of data to determine if the planned changes are effective. In the "Act" portion of the cycle, the findings from the "Check" phase are used as a basis for taking actions that institutionalize useful changes.

TQL Adaptations of the PDCA Cycle

There are several keys that are helpful in the adaptation and integration of the PDCA cycle into today's unique competitive business environment. For more detailed information I suggest you read *A Total Quality Leadership Process*

Improvement Model (Houston & Dockstader, 1993*)* and the *Systems Approach to Process Improvement* course (Rodriguez, Landau, & Konoske, 1993). These adaptations share common properties in that they:

➤ **Require empirical evidence.** In TQL, objective information takes precedence over subjective perceptions as the basis for decision-making. The identification of problems, their potential causes, and solutions must be based on objective information, not anecdotal evidence or subjective perception to guide improvement activities. The determination of causes as well as the effectiveness of efforts to improve organizational performance must be verified with data.

➤ **Use analytic tools to gain new knowledge.** Analytic methods and tools help team members to collect, organize, and interpret information. They also serve as a common language that aids in communication and decision-making within an organization. Without the discipline offered by these tools and methods, it is difficult for an organization to learn. When an organization does not learn, it risks repeating mistakes or applying the same ineffective solutions over and over again (Rodriguez, Landau, & Konoske, 1993).

➤ **Address causes of performance problems.** There are two kinds of causes of problems associated with process performance. These are known as common causes and special causes. The ability to distinguish between the two causes and take appropriate action is essential to improvement.

1. Common causes are sources of variation due to the system itself or the way the system is managed. They represent factors that are inherent and have a widespread effect on performance, such as the quality of incoming resources, training, or standard equipment or operating procedures. Addressing common causes of performance typically requires system changes.

2. Special causes are sources of variation due to isolated abnormalities or exceptional occurrences in the system; they are not a regular part of the system. Correcting the effects of special causes usually can be accomplished through problem solving. Actions taken on special causes can lead to immediate results, but actions on the common causes can generate the greatest and most lasting benefits.

➤ **Help organizations to be proactive.** By anticipating and preventing poor performance, the organization's overall effectiveness is improved and limited resources are used efficiently. The organization can also use the PDCA cycle in conjunction with strategic plans to identify and respond to new requirements.

- ➤ **Are cyclical.** As indicated above, status quo is not good enough. Changes in corporate goals, market conditions, resources, and operational constraints require organizations to continually seek out new and better ways to achieve their goals. Effective application of the PDCA cycle requires the ongoing acquisition and use of new knowledge to address emerging organizational needs.

- ➤ **Are value-focused.** Pursuing improvement through TQL does not mean quality at any cost, but rather quality at a cost the user is willing to pay. Improving corporate effectiveness begins with reducing complexity and eliminating activities that do not add value (Lean Manufacturing). Process redesign or re-engineering efforts that may follow initial improvements are designed to increase the value of the process as it relates to the company's performance. This value based orientation is fundamental to TQL.

This approach embraces a definition of TQL that addresses short and long-term organizational goals, adoption of the Deming philosophy, an implementation approach, a management structure and roles, and the application of the scientific method. Requirements for the successful use of TQL include education and training, leadership, and teamwork.

The TQL approach requires that organizational leaders begin the practice of process management in their organizations. Once implementation is underway, the leader is responsible for expanding improvement to all significant processes and ultimately the entire extended system. Then leaders can focus on setting a long term, strategic direction for the organization and systematically deploying the goals throughout the organization. In this way, the products and services can be directed at meeting the future needs of our customers in Deming's "new economic age" of the 21st century.

"Problems are only opportunities in work clothes."
Henry J. Kaiser

Chapter 7: Opportunities for Improvement

Opportunity Seeking

In some ways, I am "old school" and not always politically correct. For example, I know that we should *not* be trying to identify problems in our organizations; we should be looking for "opportunities for improvement". However, I am not one to change the name of something to match the flavor of the month leadership techniques. I know there are opportunities to do things better in our organizations and I believe and follow the Kaizen methodology for continuous improvement efforts that we have discussed. But I know there are also real problems in our organization; problems that we must identify and solve.

When it comes to identifying problems and opportunities in our organizations, I suggest following a creative problem solving process.

Creative Problem Solving Process

Step 1. Problem Formulation: The problems and challenges we face each day represent barriers to the achievement of organizational goals and objectives. The process of formulating the problem into a clear and concise statement is the most important step in the creative problem solving (ok, opportunity seeking) and decision making process. Yet far too often, it is the most neglected step. It seems everyone knows what the problem is – all you have to do is ask them! Leaders often assume that everyone knows what the problem is, so the problem never gets written down in a clear and concise statement. Since the true problem is never completely identified, we end up attacking symptoms of the problem, rather than the true problem.

Symptoms are just the visible indicators that something is wrong. How often have you heard someone say, "Boy, this place sure has a morale problem!" Perhaps, you have noticed a department has high absenteeism or high turnover. These situations are all symptoms of a deeper problem. If a doctor tries to treat symptoms of a serious disease, the patient might appear to improve temporarily, but will likely get worse in the long run. The same thing is true in this situation. A morale problem might appear to improve for a few weeks or even months; but the situation will only get worse if the true problem that caused the low morale is not identified and corrected. An excellent technique to get to the bottom or *root cause* of a situation is to ask "why" five times. The idea is that you must really dig to get past the symptoms and find the true cause. Asking why five times forces you to go beyond the superficial symptoms and get to the true causes of the problem, allowing you to see the opportunities for change and improvement.

Step 2. Understand Your Environment: All leaders and managers must develop a "feel" for the environment in which they work. At a minimum, you must be knowledgeable of changes in consumer tastes and preferences, you must be aware of changes in technology, and finally, you must know what your competition is doing. To be knowledgeable and become an expert in your chosen field, you should devote at least one hour a day to relevant reading material. When a manager has a "feel" for what is going on around them they can recognize problems and see opportunities that might otherwise be overlooked. Decision makers, must have a clear understanding of the resources that are available to them and the constraints that they must overcome. This information will become clear when you develop an in-depth understanding of your environment.

As we begin to understand our business environment we will gain an in-depth understanding of both our resources and our constraints. Resources and constraints typically fall into the same categories of: time, money, and people. Understanding of our constraints is vital as it allows us to budget them appropriately in order to maximize their usefulness.

Step 3. Development of Alternatives: As a decision maker you want to develop as many different alternatives to a situation as you can. Also, at this point, you want to focus on creativity. One of the best ways to gain creativity and improve the "buy-in" from your team is to get them involved! Learn to have frequent brainstorming sessions with your team. The team knows where the problems/opportunities are so harness their collective mind!

I want to review just a few key ideas about brainstorming to keep in mind. First, write every idea on a flip chart or white board so everyone can see them. Second, remember the focus here is on *quantity of ideas*, not the quality of the ideas. Encourage freewheeling and tag-on ideas. And remember, no evaluation of the ideas at this point (that comes later). No matter how silly the suggestion seems, keep that to yourself and build on it – but do not bash it out loud!

Step 4. Determine the Best Alternative: Evaluation and selection of alternatives is the very heart of the decision making, problem solving process. The first step is to determine which alternatives are feasible. Many of the alternatives generated during the brainstorming secession will not be realistic. Some of the alternatives will cost too much or perhaps take too much time to implement or too much labor.

After you have determined the feasible alternatives you must evaluate them. Evaluate the feasible alternatives with respect to two factors: quality and acceptability. When considering the quality of an alternative, think about both the efficiency and effectiveness of the alternative. According to Peter Drucker, efficiency means doing things right and effectiveness means doing the right things. *The efficient alternative is worthless if it is ineffective!*

Also, the chosen alternative must be acceptable. *Failure to be acceptable is a key reason why the chosen alternative will fail in the long run.* One excellent way to insure acceptability is to get your team involved in the decision making process by using the brainstorming technique.

Step 5. Implementation and Feedback: Only time will tell whether or not the selected alternative was the correct decision. You must realize that most all decisions made by the business leaders of today are made under conditions of risk and uncertainty. No one can know all of the various factors about any situation. For this reason, during the implementation of a decision, new information may come into light. *Chisel the decision in sand not stone!* Remember to be flexible, be ready to change or modify the plan as necessary. Keep the lines of communication open between yourself and the people who are implementing the decision. Keep your team involved. Use the feedback that they can provide you.

If the selected alternative does not correct the predicament, ask yourself if the problem was correctly identified. If the problem was correctly identified, perhaps another alternative might be examined.

Process Improvement

As previously discussed, organizations are systems (See Figure 3, page 24) and they are composed of processes necessary to achieve organizational goals. Far too often the successful company has grown so fast that they are now doing things very inefficiently and the processes are in need of improvements. Or consider the company that is not as successful as it could be, certainly this company is in dire need of improvement!

True and ongoing "process improvement" (page 15) means making things better, not just fighting fires or managing crises. It means setting aside the customary practice of blaming people for problems or failures. It is a way of looking at how we can do our work better. Caution should be exercised when we take a simple problem-solving approach or simply try to fix what's broken, we may never discover or understand the root cause of the difficulty (remember, use the 5 whys to find the root cause). Process improvement changes should be planned for and implemented continuously, not done in a haphazard fashion.

When we are truly engaged in ongoing process improvement, we seek to learn what causes things to happen in a process and to use this knowledge to reduce variation (quality improvements), remove activities that contribute no value to the product or service produced (lean corporate culture), and improve customer satisfaction. A team examines all of the factors affecting the process: the materials used in the process, the methods and machines used to transform the materials into a product or service, and the people who perform the work (see Chapter 9, Cause-and-Effect Diagram).

Remember our basic PDCA and use it to keep your process improvements efforts on track.

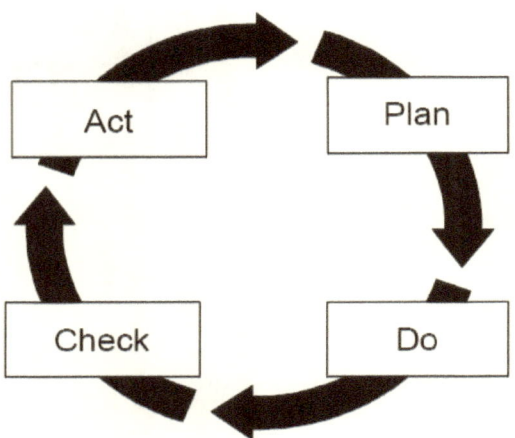

Plan: Select the process to be improved & identify a root cause of the problem. Establish a well-defined process improvement objective. Create a Flowchart for a simple process or a Current State Map from more complex processes. (The next chapter has detailed information on Flowcharting, Chapter 11 details Current and Future State Maps.)

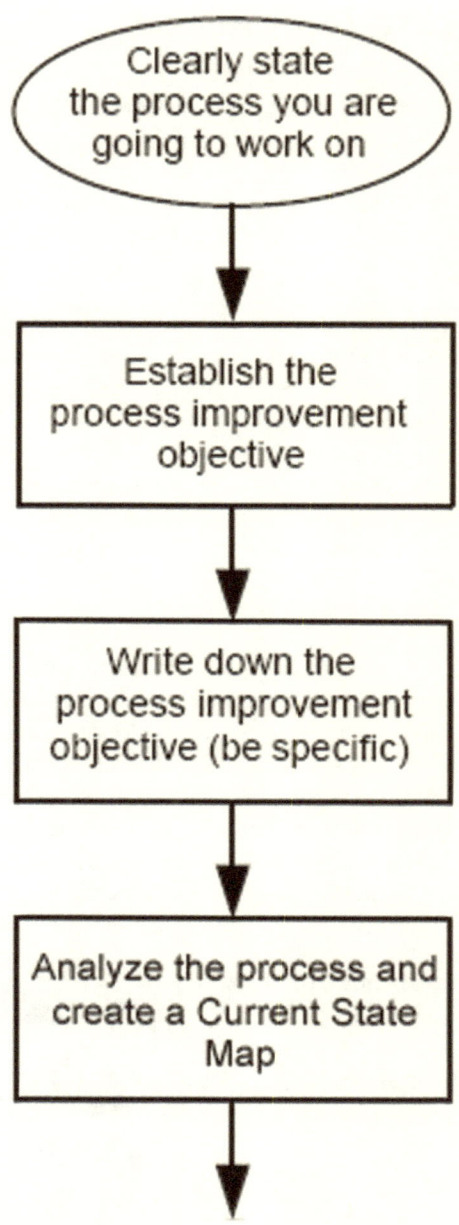

PROCESS SELECTION WORKSHEET

STATE PROBLEMS OR EXPECTATIONS IDENTIFIED BY INTERVIEWING YOUR CUSTOMERS:

a. _____

b. _____

c. _____

d. _____

PLACE A CHECKMARK NEXT TO ALL OF THE ITEMS THAT APPLY TO YOUR PROCESS:

___1. The process can be defined. (Be careful not to pick something too big. It should be possible to complete the improvement effort within 90 days.)

___2. A problem in the process occurs frequently. (A Pareto analysis may be helpful.)

___3. The problem area is well-known and has visibility in the command, work center, or office.

___4. Improvement of this process is important to the command.

___5. People will appreciate it if the process is improved.

___6. There is a good chance of success in improving the process.

___7. No one else is currently working on this process.

___8. Required changes can be put into effect with little or no outside help.

___9. This is truly a process improvement effort, not just an attempt to impose a solution on a problem.

NOTE: IF YOU HAVE SELECTED AN APPROPRIATE PROCESS, YOU SHOULD BE ABLE TO CHECK ALL OF THE ITEMS ABOVE.

Develop a plan to implement a change in the process to reduce or eliminate the root cause.

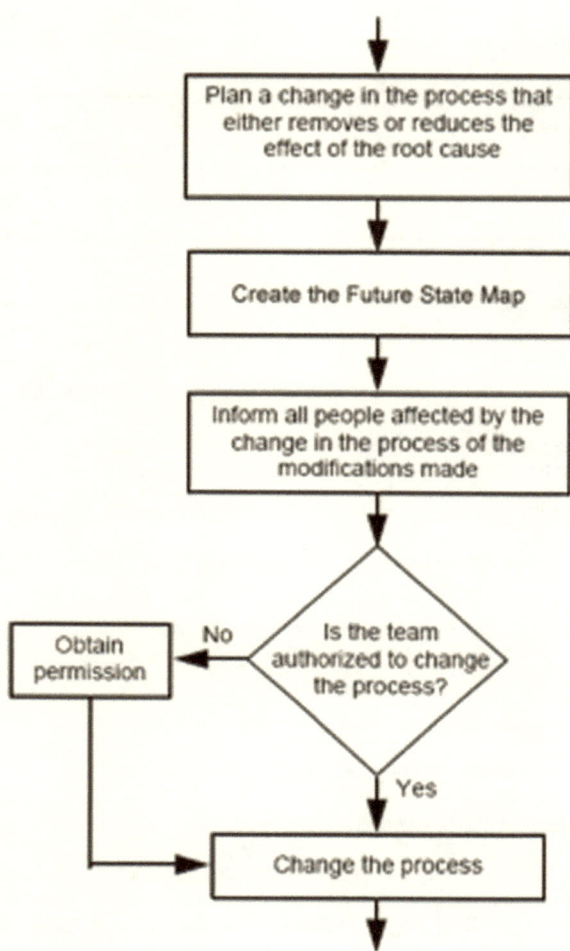

Do: The goals are to prove the effectiveness of the change, avoid widespread failure, and maintain support.

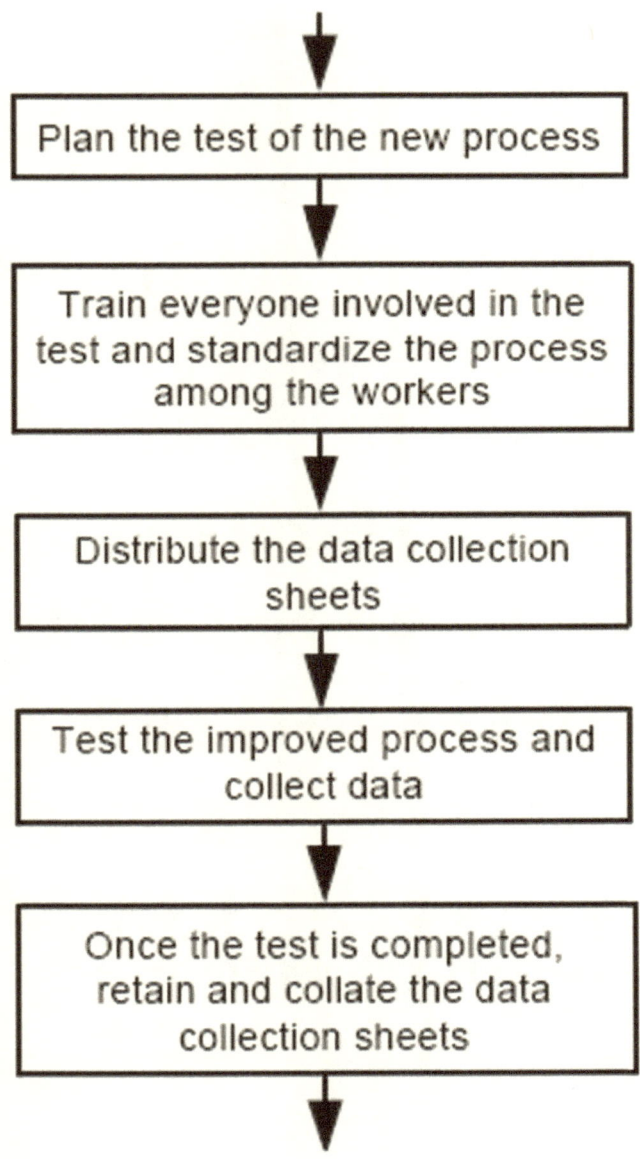

Check: The team modified the process based on the improvement plan and conducted a test. During the test of the new procedure, data were collected. Data may be collected using check sheets and controls charts. Now the team checks whether the expected results were achieved.

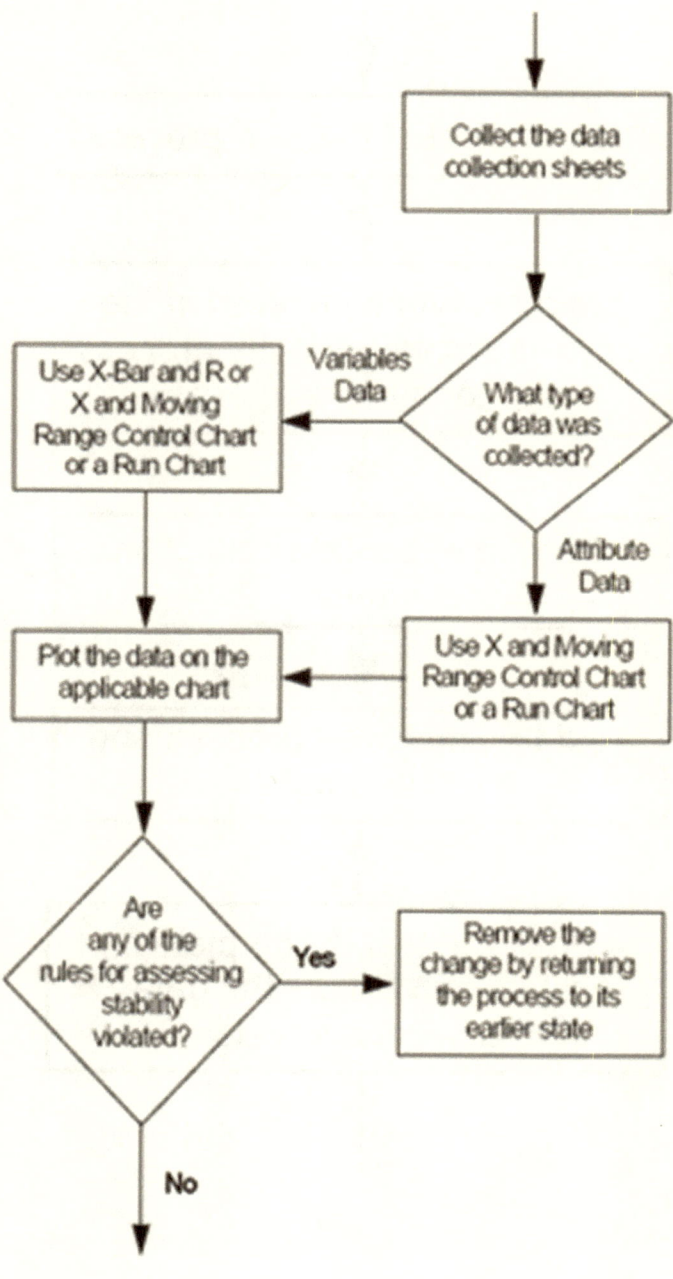

Act: Team decides whether or not to implement the change on a full-scale basis and then makes presentation of results to Quality Council.

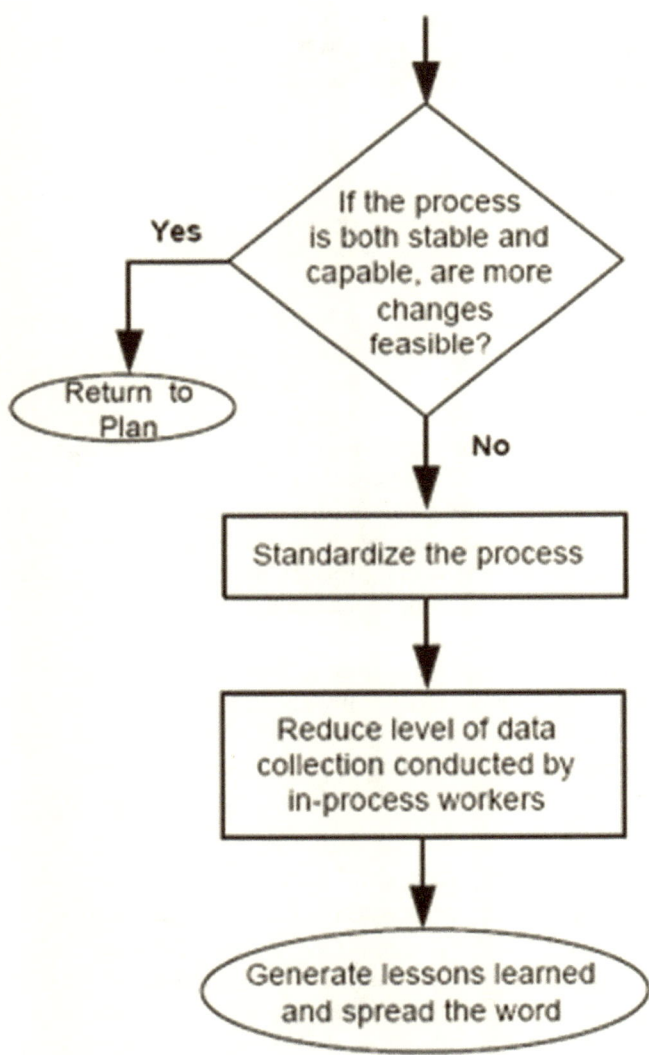

Chapter 8:
Data Collection

Why collect data?

Data Collection helps your team to assess the health of your process. To do so, you must identify the key quality characteristics you will measure, how you will measure them, and what you will do with the data you collect.

What exactly is a key quality characteristic? It is a characteristic of the product or service produced by a process that customers have determined is important to them. (Remember the basic idea of fitness for use?) Key quality characteristics are such things as the speed of delivery of a service, the finish on a set of stainless steel shelves, the precision with which an electronic component is calibrated, or the effectiveness of an administrative response to a tasking by higher authority. Every product or service has multiple key quality characteristics. When you are selecting processes to improve, you need to find out the processes, or process steps, that produce the characteristics your customers perceive as important to product quality.

Data Collection is nothing more than planning for and obtaining useful information on key quality characteristics produced by your process. However, simply collecting data does not ensure that you will obtain relevant or specific enough data to tell you what is occurring in your process. The key issue is not: How do we collect data? Rather, it is: How do we obtain *useful* data?

Why do we need to collect data?

Every process improvement effort relies on data to provide a factual basis for making decisions throughout the Plan-Do-Check-Act cycle. Data Collection enables a team to formulate and test working assumptions about a process and develop information that will lead to the improvement of the key quality characteristics of the product or service. Data Collection improves your decision-making by helping you focus on objective information about what is happening in the process, rather than subjective opinions. In other words, I think the problem is... becomes... The data indicate the problem is...

Why we need a well-defined Data Collection process?

For your team to collect data uniformly, you will need to develop a Data Collection plan. The elements of the plan must be clearly and unambiguously defined — operationally defined. An Operational Definition is a definition that gives communicable meaning to a concept by specifying how the concept is measured and applied within a particular set of circumstances. (Deming, 1986)

Why we need Operational Definitions

"Our troubles are over, coach. I found us a 7-footer ..."

Why does a team need Operational Definitions in order to collect useful data? Let's say three people are collecting data on the time it takes to perform a certain process step. Unless the exact moment when each action begins and the exact moment when it ends are operationally defined, each data collector will observe and record data based on his or her own understanding of the situation. The Data Collection process will not be standardized or consistent. You will have collected data, but it probably won't be much good to you. Worse yet, you may make changes to your process based on flawed information.

Data Collection can involve a multitude of decisions by data collectors. When you prepare your Data Collection plan, you should try to eliminate as many subjective choices as possible by operationally defining the parameters needed to do the job correctly. It may be as simple as establishing separate criteria and a specific way to judge when a step begins and when it ends. Your data collectors will then have a standard operating procedure to use during their Data Collection activities.

When should we develop a Data Collection plan?

You should develop your Data Collection plan during the Plan Phase of the Plan-Do-Check-Act (PDCA) cycle. The PDCA cycle provides a framework for you to build an understanding of your process and how to obtain and interpret data that will lead to real process improvement. Although they can be time-consuming, planning sessions are extremely important because this is when you establish the guidance that helps you obtain the right data.

What questions does Data Collection answer?

Your team needs to develop the answers to the following questions as the basis for a sound Data Collection plan:

➢ *Why do we want the data?* What will we do with the data after we have collected them? The team must decide on a purpose for collecting the data. In the Plan Phase, your team should develop a working hypothesis which will serve as a guide to future investigation of the process. This hypothesis is an assumption based on already existing data and observations, such as your process Flowcharts, Value Stream Mapping, or a Cause-and-Effect Diagram the team has prepared. You develop working assumptions and collect data to determine the process changes that will improve the key quality characteristics of your product or service. Your proposed change should be stated as an "If . . . then" statement. IF we change Step X in our process by doing . . ., we believe we will THEN improve Y, which is a key quality characteristic of our product or service.

➢ *Where will we collect the data?* The location where data are collected must be identified clearly. This is not an easy step unless you tackle it from the following perspective:

  o Refer to the Flowcharts or Value Stream Mapping which depict both the current ("as is") state of the process and the proposed ("should be") state of the process after it has been modified. Focus on the process steps where the key quality characteristic you are trying to improve is produced.

  o Collect data from these process steps. You must collect data twice. First, you collect baseline data before you make any changes in your process. These baseline data will serve as a yardstick against which to compare the results of the process after changes have been made. Then, you must collect data after the change has been imposed on the process. To compare the before and after process, you will probably want to translate your data into graphic form using a Pareto Chart, Run Chart, or Histogram.

- o Collect data on the key quality characteristic of the product or service at the end of your process. Again, before and after data must be collected. The comparison of before and after data validates whether the change actually improved the output of the process.

➢ *What type of data will we collect?* In general, data can be classified into two major types: attribute data and variables data.

- o Attribute data give you counts representing the presence or absence of a characteristic or defect. These counts are based on the occurrence of discrete events. As an example, if you are concerned with timely delivery of parts by your store keepers, you could develop a procedure that would give you a count of the number of supply parts they deliver on time and the number they deliver late (defects). This would give you attribute data, but it would not tell you how late a late delivery actually was. Two factors help determine whether attribute data will be useful:

    - ▪ Operational Definitions. You need to operationally define exactly what constitutes a defect. For the data collected to be useful, you would have to operationally define late.
    - ▪ Area of Opportunity. For counts to be useful, they must come from a well-defined area of opportunity. You obtain a single count, or value, from each sample, or area of opportunity. For example, if you are collecting data on the number of defective gizmos received in each shipment of 200, the area of opportunity is the 200-gizmo shipment. The number of defective gizmo in the shipment gives you one count, or data point.

- o Variables data are based on measurement of a key quality characteristic produced by the process. Such measurements might include length, width, time, weight, or temperature, to name a few. Continuing with the parts delivery example, you could collect variables data by tabulating the time it took to process an incoming supply request from receipt to validation of the Stock Number (SN); or the time from validation of the SN to identification of the stock bin where the part is located; or the time required to post the obligation in the Receiving Log; or the total time from receipt of the request to delivery of the part. This measurement, time, could be used to determine how timely or late the deliveries were.

➤ *Who will collect the data?* Many teams struggle with this question, but the answer is simple: Those closest to the data—the process workers—the people on the front line should collect the data. These people have the best opportunity to record the results. They also know the process best and can easily detect when problems occur. But remember, the people who are going to collect the data *need training* on how to do it, and the resources necessary to obtain the information, such as time, paper, pencils, and measurement tools.

➤ *How do we collect the right data?* You need to remember that you are collecting data for the purpose of improving the process, not the product it produces. Clearly, you want to collect the data that best describe the situation at hand. If you are going to use the data to make predictions about the performance of the process, you should collect small samples at regular intervals — let's say 4 or 5 units every other hour or each day. Since it is important to collect those 4 or 5 units in a short interval of time, you may want to use consecutive units or every other unit.

But remember, the cost of obtaining the data, the availability of data, and the consequences of decisions made on the basis of the data should be taken into consideration when determining how much data should be obtained and how frequently it should be collected.

What Data Collection problems should we avoid?

Remembering that data form the basis for the effective, unemotional communication without which no process improvement effort can succeed, you need to avoid two significant problems associated with Data Collection.

Problem 1 - Failure to establish Operational Definitions. You need to define, not simply identify, the following:

➤ When and how often you will collect the data
➤ How you will collect the data
➤ Units of measurement you will use in collecting the data
➤ The criteria for defects
➤ How you will handle multiple defects on single products

If you haven't thought about these issues, your Data Collection process may be doomed from the start. This is especially true when more than one person is collecting data. What is meaningful to one worker might not be to another. You have to take the time to develop adequate, clear-cut definitions, and train each collector to use those definitions.

Problem 2 - Adding bias to the Data Collection process. You can never eliminate bias, but it is important to minimize it. Here are some ways your data can be biased:

➤ The process of collecting the data may affect the process being studied. If you are trying to make a process faster, taking data may either speed it up or slow it down.

    o On the one hand, the workers may speed up the way they work in the process, thus skewing the data in their favor. This may occur if they have a perception that the variables data they are collecting will show that they could be more efficient, productive, or effective. Once the Data Collection effort ceases, they may return to their old pace of operations.

    o On the other hand, the burden of Data Collection may cause a slowdown in the natural flow of the process. If such events are affecting your improvement efforts, you need to alter your Data Collection plan.

➤ The attitudes and perceptions of the data collectors can affect what they see and how they record data. If there is a sense that the data will be used against them, workers may use the data collection process to cast a favorable light on the process being studied. You have to get past this fear in order to collect accurate data. You might want to consider an amnesty program. Data collectors need to be assured that their leaders realize that the data gathered in the past may have been tainted by fear. This requires a commitment by your leadership that the new information — possibly less glowing or flattering—will not be compared against old data or their perception of how your process operated in the past.

➤ Failure to follow the established Data Collection procedures can add errors to the data. This bias occurs when the Data Collection instructions, training, or checksheets are not adequately prepared and tested in an operational environment. You need to conduct initial training on Data Collection and then perform a small-scale Data Collection trial to see if it all works smoothly. The small-scale trial may uncover some problems which need to be ironed out before you can actively pursue a larger scale Data Collection effort. The trial may reveal that you need to make a minor change in the checksheet to make it clearer or easier to use, or that additional training on Operational Definitions is required to calibrate the eyes of the data collectors.

➤ Data may be missing. Don't assume that missing data will show the same results as the data you collected. The fact that the data are missing is a clue that they may be different from the rest. It is best to number the checksheets sequentially to make it easier to verify that you have them all and that all the required samples have been taken.

What do we use to collect data?

Data are frequently collected using checksheets — structured forms that enable you to collect and organize data systematically. Because each checksheet is used for collecting and recording data unique to a specific process, it can be constructed in whatever shape, size, and format are appropriate for the Data Collection task at hand.

Checksheets have three important uses:
1. Record information on the key quality characteristics of your process for analysis using tools such as a Pareto Charts, Histograms, and Run Charts.
2. Provide a historical record of the process over time.
3. Introduce Data Collection methods to workers and supervisors who may not be familiar or comfortable with collecting data as a regular part of their jobs.

What types of checksheets are there?

The most common types of checksheets collect data either in tabular form or in a location-style format. Occasionally you may encounter a graphic-style checksheet. No matter which type of checksheet you are using, make sure that it is designed to be clear, complete, and user friendly.

Tabular format A tabular checksheet — also known as a "tally sheet"— is easy for you and your team to use when you simply want to count how often something happens or to record a measurement. Depending on the type of data required, the data collector simply makes a checkmark in a column to indicate the presence of a characteristic, or records a measurement, such as temperature

July								
DEFECT	12	13	14	15	16	17	18	TOTAL
WRONG NSN	II	I	II	I	I	I		8
FAULTY MATERIAL	I	II		I		I		5
PMS NOT DONE	II	III	II	III	I	III	II	16
INSTALL PROBLEMS				I		I		2

Figure 8 Tabular Format

in degrees centigrade, weight in pounds, diameter in inches, or time in seconds. (See Figure 8)

Location format A location checksheet allows you to mark a diagram showing the exact physical location of a defect or characteristic. An insurance adjuster's pictorial claim form detailing your latest bumper bruise is an example of a location checksheet. (See Figure 9)

DATE: _____   COMMENTS: _____

DEPT: _____   _____

LOT NUMBER: _____

NUMBER OF BURRS: _____

INSPECTOR: _____

DEFECT LOCATIONS

Location of burrs on a special gear marked with an X.

Figure 9 Location Format

Graphic format Another way of collecting data is by using a graphic form of checksheet. It is specifically designed so that the data can be recorded and displayed at the same time. Using this checksheet format, you can record raw data by plotting them directly onto a graph-like chart. Figure 10 is an example of a checksheet which also produces a Run Chart as the individual data points are plotted and the adjacent points are joined with a straight line.

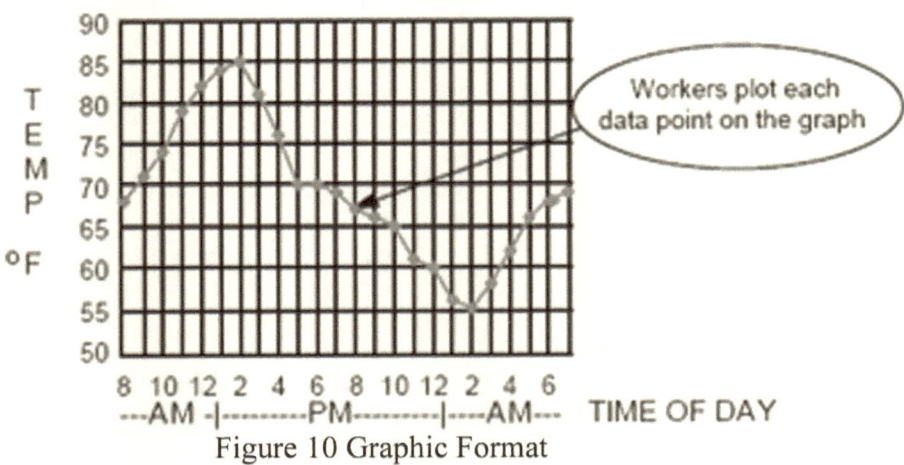

Figure 10 Graphic Format

How do we develop _useful_ Checksheets?

There is no standardized format that you can apply to all checksheets. Instead, each checksheet is a form tailored to collect the information needed to improve a specific process. Remember, a well-designed checksheet is the launching pad for an effective analysis in which data become meaningful information. With that in mind, here are some guidelines to help you develop useful forms:

- ➤ Involve the process workers in developing the checksheet for their process.
- ➤ Label all columns clearly. Organize your form so that the data are recorded in the sequence seen by a person viewing the process. This reduces the possibility of data being recorded in the wrong column or not being recorded.
- ➤ Make the form user-friendly. Make sure the checksheet can be easily understood and used by all of the workers who are recording data.
    - o Include brief instructions on the back of the form.
    - o Create a format that gives you the most information with the least amount of effort. For example, design your checksheet so that data can be recorded using only a checkmark, slant mark, number, or letter.
    - o Provide enough space for the collectors to record all of the data.
    - o Designate a place for recording the date and time the data were collected. These elements are required when the data are used with Run Charts or other tools which require the date and time of each observation.
    - o Provide a place to enter the name of the individual collecting the data.
    - o Allow enough space so data collectors can write in comments on unusual events. This information could be entered on the back of the form.

Now let's work through an example that illustrate how to determine where to collect baseline data and how to use checksheets to capture them.

Pharmacy Waiting Time: A team of hospital employees working in a Medical Clinic are attempting to improve service in the pharmacy by decreasing the time patients wait for their prescriptions (i.e., the key quality characteristic). The desired end state is reduced waiting time for the patients. The team proceeds as follows:

- ➤ They develop a Flowchart of the process (Figure 11).
- ➤ After examining the Flowchart and discussing the steps, they conclude that a possible bottleneck in their process occurs at the point where a

prescription is filled by the pharmacist. This is supported by general observations of team members.

➢ They develop a hypothesis along with their "should be" Flowchart.
➢ They opt to take baseline data using a checksheet to assess both the time required for the pharmacist's actions and the overall time required to process the prescription, as depicted in Figure 12.

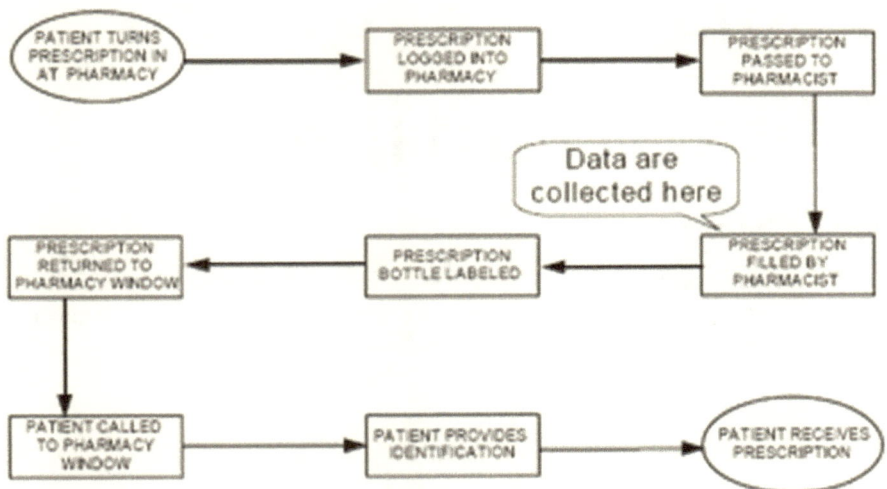

Figure 11 Pharmacy Waiting Time Flow Chart

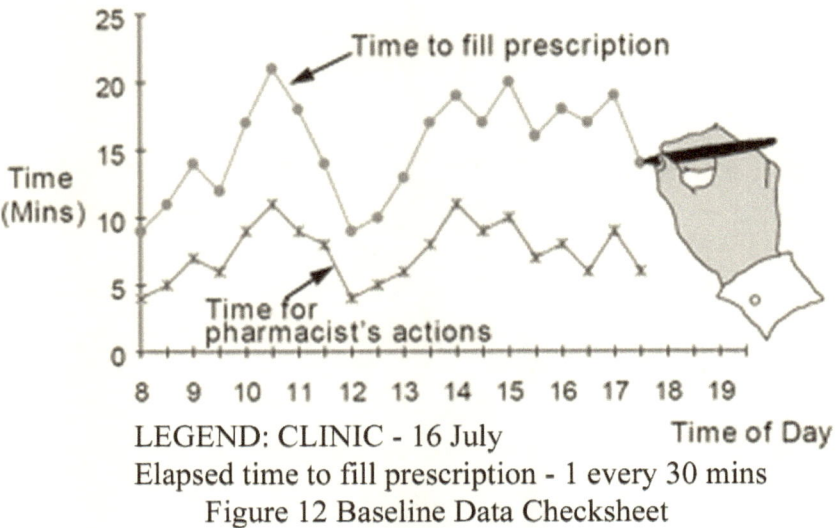

LEGEND: CLINIC - 16 July   Time of Day
Elapsed time to fill prescription - 1 every 30 mins
Figure 12 Baseline Data Checksheet

Chapter 9:
Tools for Problem Identification

Flow Charts

One of the most basic tools is that of flow charting. This tool allows you visually see all of the steps in a process. We used flowcharts in chapter seven to illustrate the steps in the PDCA cycle. This works well when the process is simple; however, there are some limitations if the process is complex. Below is an example of a simple flow chart.

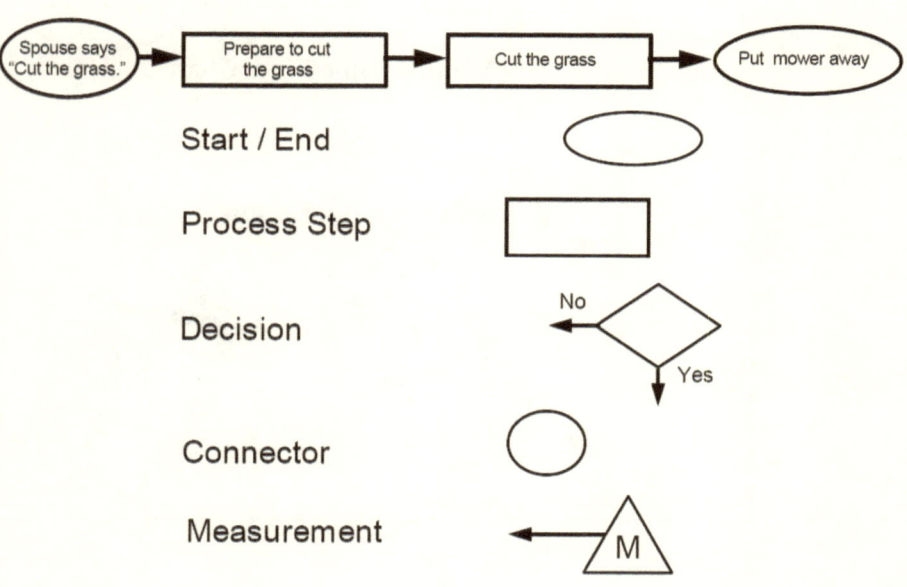

The problem is, as we take a more detailed look at the project we see there are many more than just four steps!

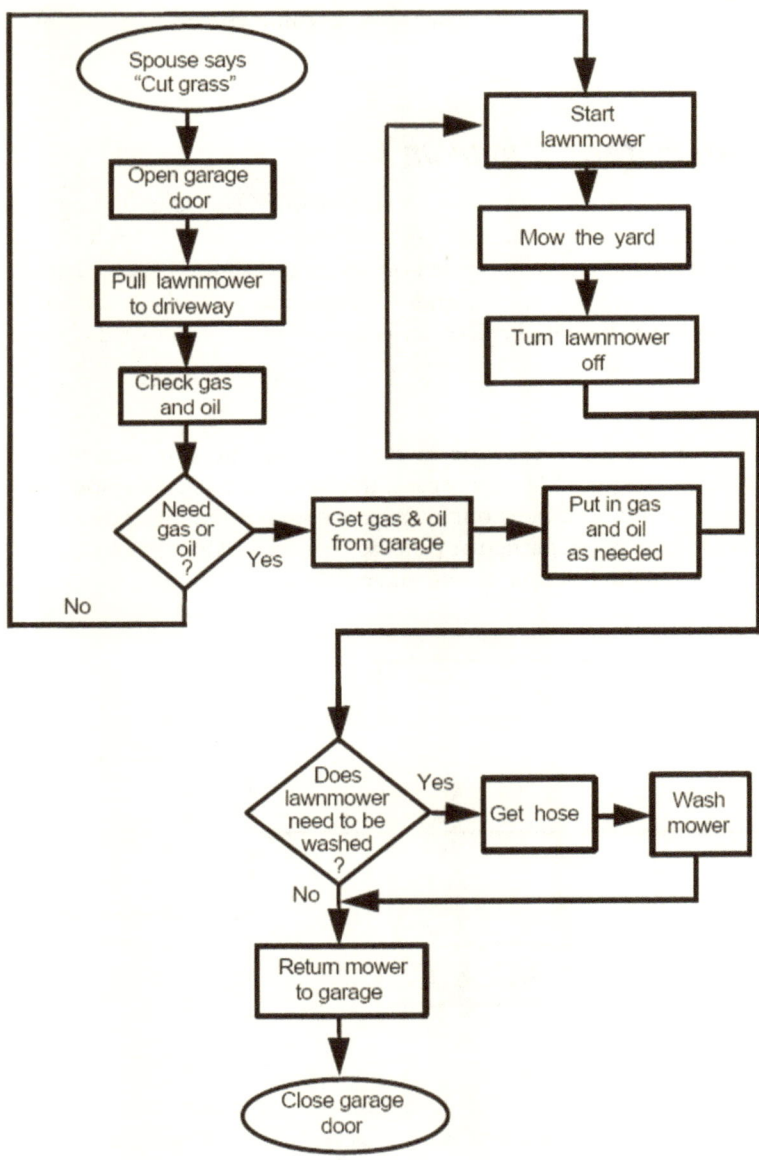

The flow chart gives us a picture of the process. It's a great visual representation of a process, yet something is still missing. What about time, motion, and information flow! To enhance flowcharts we create Current and Future State Maps. This technique is called Value Stream Mapping and is from

Lean Manufacturing. Value Stream Mapping allows us to consider the aforementioned elements and looks at areas where the process can be improved. Lean Manufacturing is all about identifying and eliminating the waste in our processes. We'll take a closer look at Value Stream Mapping in Chapter 11, Thinking Lean.

Cause-and-Effect Diagram

A Cause-and-Effect Diagram is a tool that helps identify, sort, and display possible causes of a specific problem or quality characteristic. It graphically illustrates the relationship between a given outcome and all the factors that influence the outcome. This type of diagram is sometimes called an "Ishikawa diagram" because it was invented by Kaoru Ishikawa, or a "fishbone diagram' because of the way it looks.

Constructing a Cause-and-Effect Diagram can help you and your team when you need to identify the possible root causes, the basic reasons, for a specific effect, problem, or condition. Sort out and relate some of the interactions among the factors affecting a particular process or effect. Analyze existing problems so that corrective action can be taken.

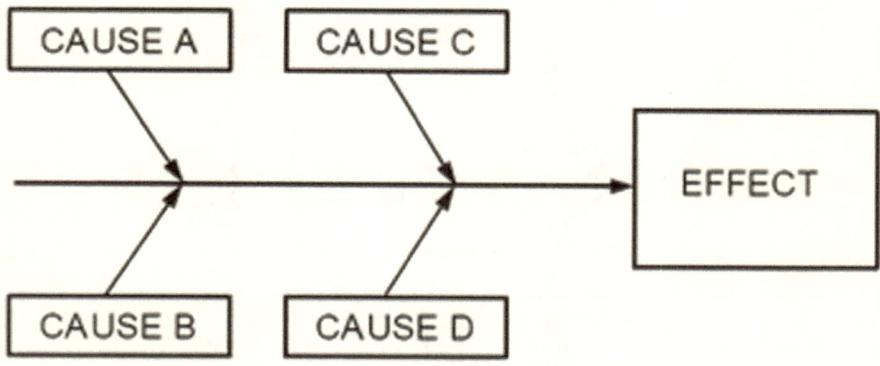

When you develop a Cause-and-Effect Diagram, you are constructing a structured, pictorial display of a list of causes organized to show their relationship to a specific effect. Notice that the diagram has a *cause* side and an *effect* side. The steps for constructing and analyzing a Cause-and-Effect Diagram are outlined on the following pages.

Begin to identify the causes than lead to the observed effect. Most causes can be grouped along the following lines.

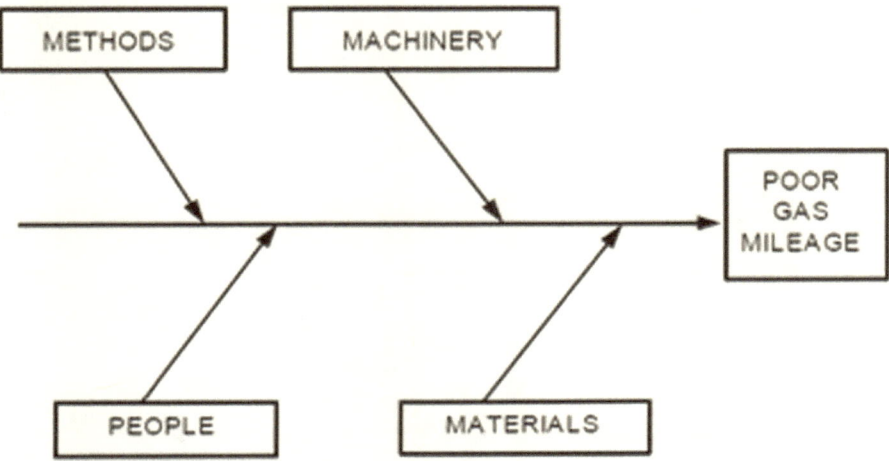

For each major branch, identify other specific factors which may be the CAUSES of the EFFECT and attach them as sub-branches.

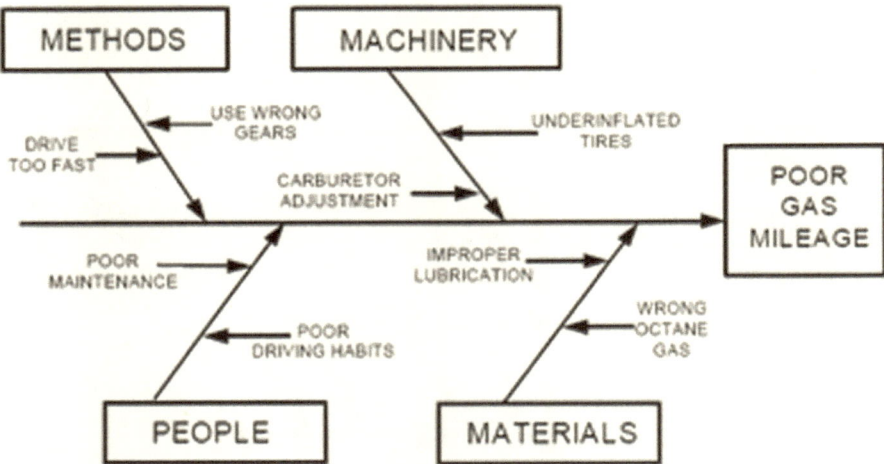

Identify increasingly more detailed levels of causes and continue organizing them under related causes or categories. You can do this by asking a series of why questions.

Q: Why was Maintenance Poor?
A: Lack of money
A: No awareness
Q: Why was Wrong Octane Gas used?
A: Didn't know recommended octane
Q: Why wasn't recommended octane known?
A: No owner's manual

Continue to refine your Cause and Effect Chart by adding more detail based on your previous analysis. For the sake of clarity, I have focused in on the People and Methods aspects.

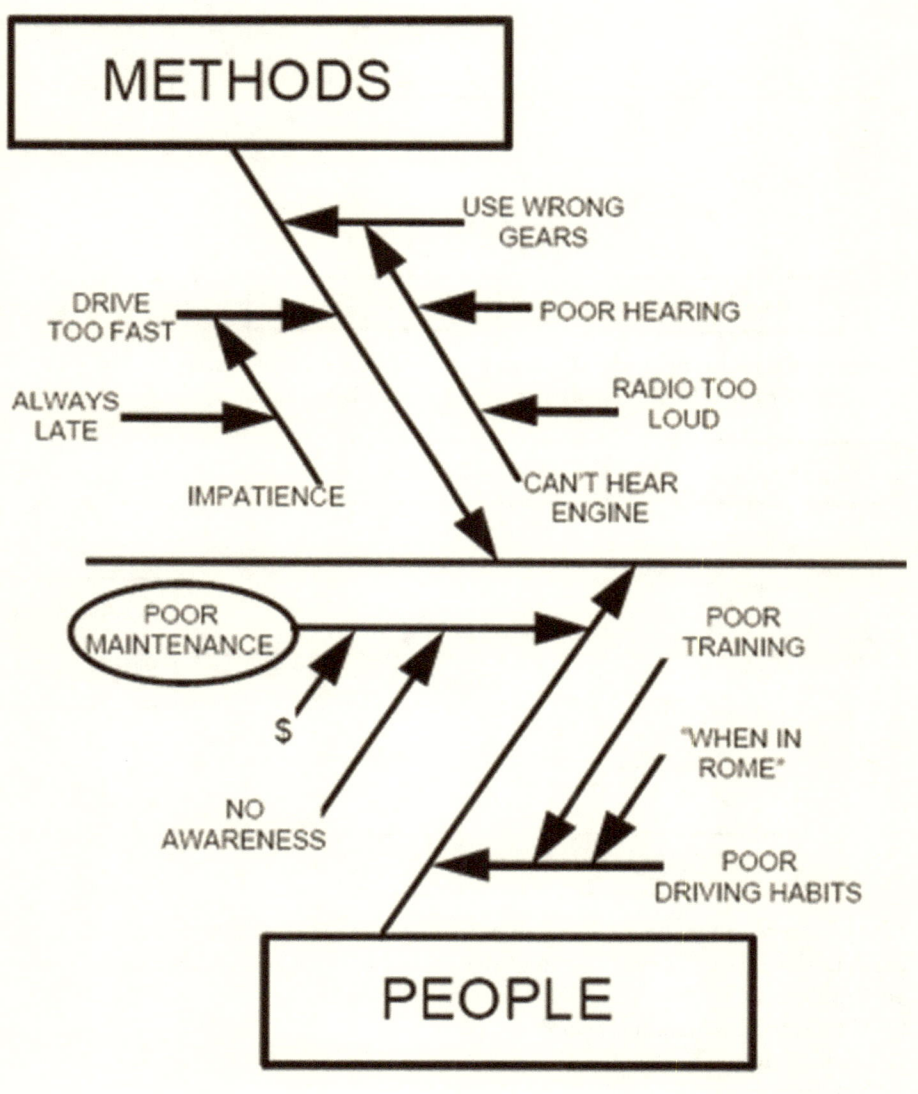

Analyze the diagram you've just created. This analysis helps you identify causes that warrant further investigation. Look at the "balance" of your diagram, checking for comparable levels of detail for most of the categories. For example, a thick cluster of items in one area may indicate a need for further study. A main category having only a few specific causes may indicate a need for further identification of causes. If several major branches have only a few sub-branches, you may need to combine them under a single category.

Look for causes that appear repeatedly. These may represent root causes. Also, look for what you can measure in each cause so you can quantify the effects of any changes you make. Most importantly, identify and circle the causes that you can take action on.

Let's analyze the diagram we have been constructing.

- The level of detail is pretty well balanced.
- No causes are repeated.
- Poor Maintenance appears to be a cause for which we could develop measurements.
- Moreover, Poor Maintenance appears to be a cause that we can take action on.
- It is circled in to earmark it for further investigation.

What is a Run Chart?

A Run Chart is the most basic tool used to display how a process performs over time. It is a line graph of data points plotted in *chronological order*—that is, the sequence in which process events occurred. These data points represent measurements, counts, or percentages of process output. Run Charts are used to assess and achieve process stability by highlighting signals of *special causes of variation*.

Why should teams use Run Charts?

Using Run Charts can help you determine whether your process is *stable* (free of special causes), consistent, and predictable. Unlike other tools, such as Pareto Charts or Histograms, Run Charts display data in the sequence in which they occurred. *This enables you to visualize how your process is performing and helps you to detect signals of special causes of variation.*

A Run Chart also allows you to present some simple statistics related to the process:

> **Median:** *The middle value of the data presented.* You will use it as the Centerline on your Run Chart.

> **Range:** *The difference between the largest and smallest values in the data.* You will use it in constructing the Y-axis of your Run Chart.

You can benefit from using a Run Chart whenever you need a graphical tool to help.

➤ Understand variation in process performance so you can improve it.

➤ Analyze data for patterns that are not easily seen in tables or spreadsheets.

➤ Monitor process performance over time to detect signals of changes.

➤ Communicate how a process performed during a specific time period.

What are the parts of a Run Chart?

As you can see in Figure 13, a Run Chart is made up of seven parts:

1. **Title:** The title briefly describes the information displayed in the Run Chart.

2. **Vertical or Y-Axis:** This axis is a scale which shows you the magnitude of the measurements represented by the data.

3. **Horizontal or X-Axis:** This axis shows you when the data were collected. It *always* represents the sequence in which the events of the process occurred.

4. **Data Points:** Each point represents an individual measurement.

5. **Centerline:** The line drawn at the median value on the Y-axis is called the Centerline. (Finding the median value is Step 3 in constructing a Run Chart.)

6. **Legend:** Additional information that documents how and when the data were collected should be entered as the legend.

7. **Data Table:** This is a sequential listing of the data being charted.

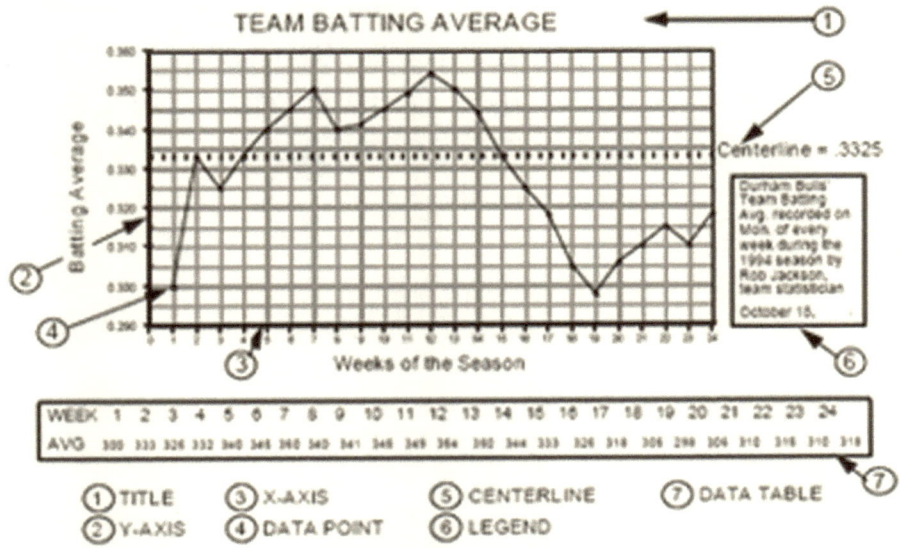

Figure 13 Parts of a Run Chart

How is a Run Chart constructed?

Step 1 - List the data. List the data you have collected in the sequence in which it occurred. You may want to refer to the Data Collection module for information on defining the purpose for the data and collecting it.

Step 2 - Order the data and determine the range To order the data, list it from the lowest value to the highest. Determine the *range* — the difference between the highest and lowest values.

Step 3 - Calculate the median Once the data have been listed from the lowest to the highest value, count off the data points and determine the *middle* point in the list of measurements — the point that divides the series of data in half.

If the count is an odd number, the middle is an odd number with an equal number of points on either side of it. If you have nine measurements, for example, the median is the fifth value. If the count is an even number, average the two middle measurements to determine the median value. For example, for 10 measurements, the median is the average of the fifth and sixth values. To determine the average, just add them together and divide by two. Now let's continue with the remaining steps.

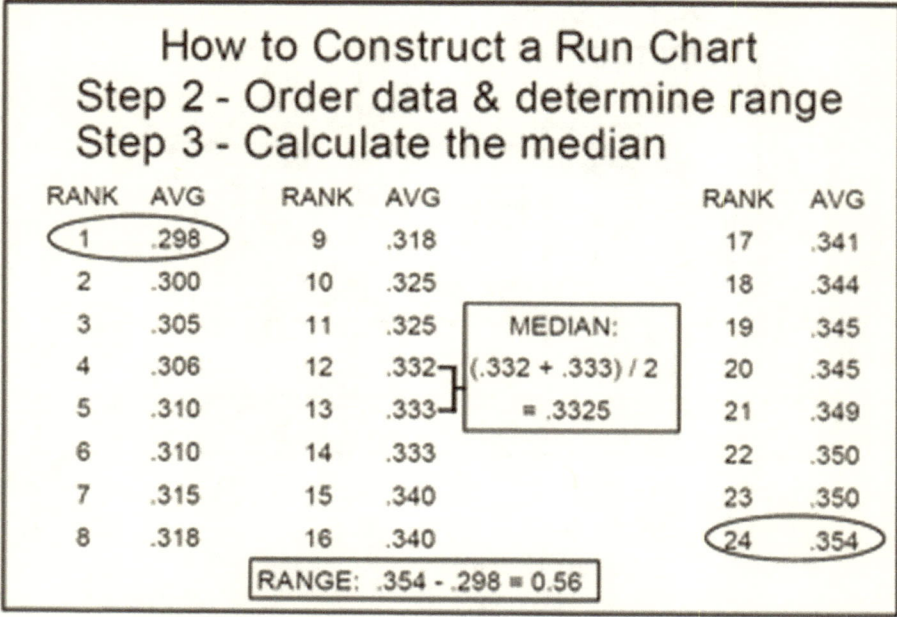

Figure 14 How to Construct a Run Chart

Step 4 - Construct the Y-Axis. Center the Y-Axis at the median. Make the Y-axis scale 1.5 to 2 times the range.

Step 5 - Draw the Centerline. Draw a horizontal line at the median value and label it as the Centerline with its value. The median is used as the Centerline, rather than the mean, to neutralize the effect of any very large or very small values.

Step 6 - Construct the X-axis. Draw the X-axis 2 to 3 times as long as the Y-axis to provide enough space for plotting all of the data points. Enter all relevant measurements and use the full width of the X-axis.

NOTE: *One of the strengths of a Run Chart is its readability, so don't risk making it harder to interpret by putting too many measurements on one sheet.* If you have more than 40 measurements, consider continuing the chart on another page.

Step 7 - Plot the data points and connect them with straight lines.

Step 8 - Provide a Title and a Legend. Give the chart a title that identifies the process you are investigating and compose a legend that tells:

- The period of time when the data were collected

- The location where the data were collected

- The person or team who collected the data

How do we interpret a Run Chart?

Interpreting a Run Chart requires you to apply some of the *theory of variation*. You are looking for trends, runs, or cycles that indicate the presence of special causes. Expect to see *variation*. Just remember that process improvement activities are expected to produce positive results, and these sometimes cause trends or runs, so the presence of special causes of variation is not always a bad sign. *A Trend signals a special cause when there is a sequence of seven or more data points steadily increasing or decreasing with no change in direction.* When a value repeats, the trend stops. The example in Figure 15 shows a decreasing trend in lower back injuries, possibly resulting from a new "Stretch and Flex" exercise program. *When the Run Chart shows seven or more consecutive ascending or descending data points, it is a signal that a special cause may be at work and the trend must be investigated.*

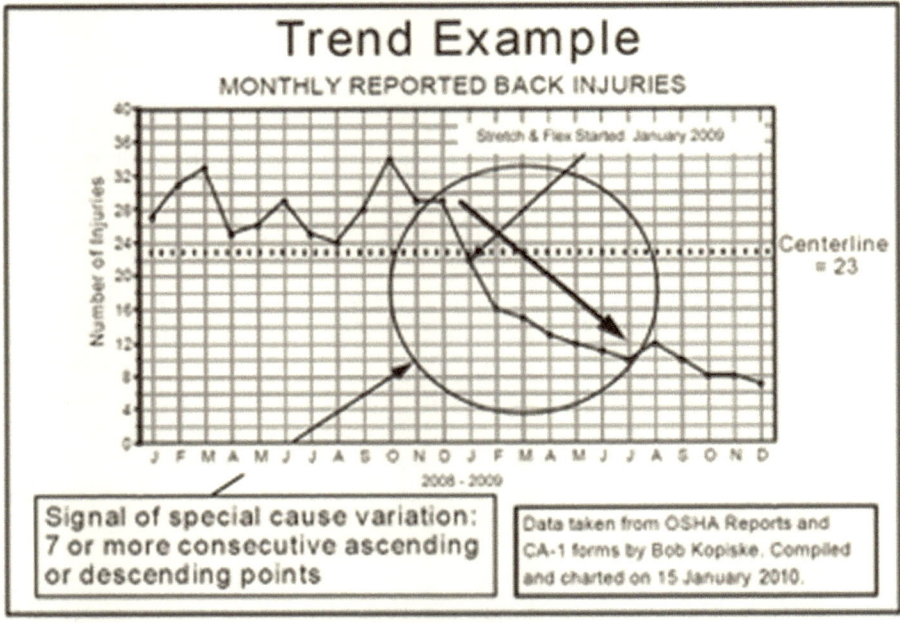

Figure 15 Run Chart: Trend Example

A Run consists of two or more consecutive data points on one side of the centerline. A run that signals a special cause is one that shows nine or more consecutive data points on one side of the centerline. In the example in Figure 16, you can see such a run occurring between 15 and 28 March. Investigation revealed that new software was responsible for the increase in duplication. This was corrected on 29 March with the introduction of a software "patch." Whenever a data point touches or crosses the centerline, a run stops and a new one starts. *When your Run Chart shows nine or more consecutive data points on one side of the centerline, it is an unusual event and should always be investigated.*

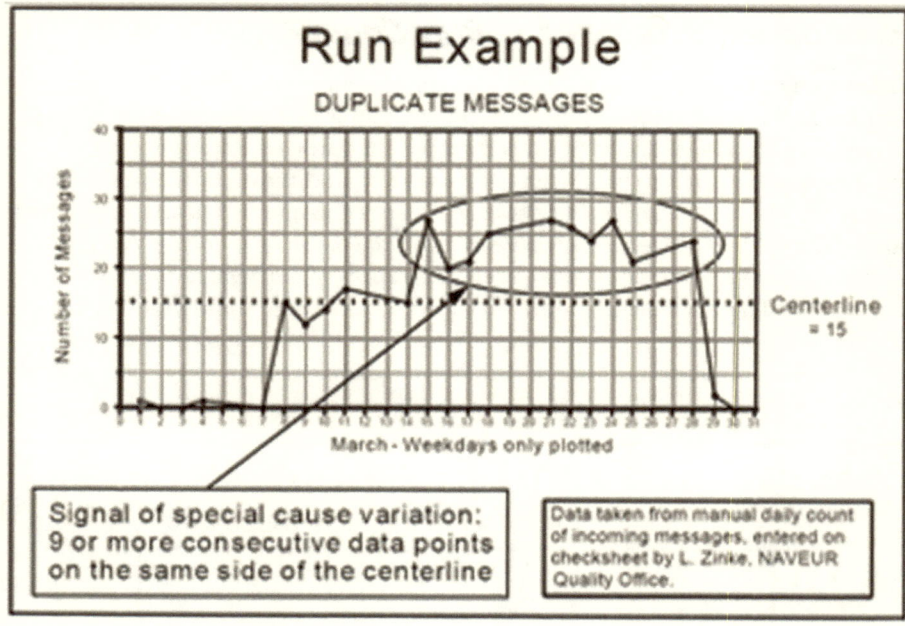

Figure 16 Run Chart: Run Example

A Cycle, or repeating pattern, is the third indication of a possible special cause. A cycle must be interpreted in the context of the process that produced it. In the example in Figure 17, an apartment manager charted data on people moving out during a four-year period and determined that there was an annual cycle. Looking at the data, it's evident that there were peaks during the summer months and valleys during the winter months. Clearly, understanding the underlying reasons why a cycle occurred in your process enables you to predict process results more accurately.

A cycle must recur at least eight times before it can be interpreted as a signal of a special cause of variation. When interpreting a cycle, remember that trends or runs might also be present, signaling other special causes of variation.

NOTE: *The absence of signals of special causes does not necessarily mean that a process is stable. Dr. Walter Shewhart suggested that a minimum of 100 observations without a signal is required before you can say that a process is in statistical control. Refer to Chapter 10, the Control Chart section for more information on this subject.*

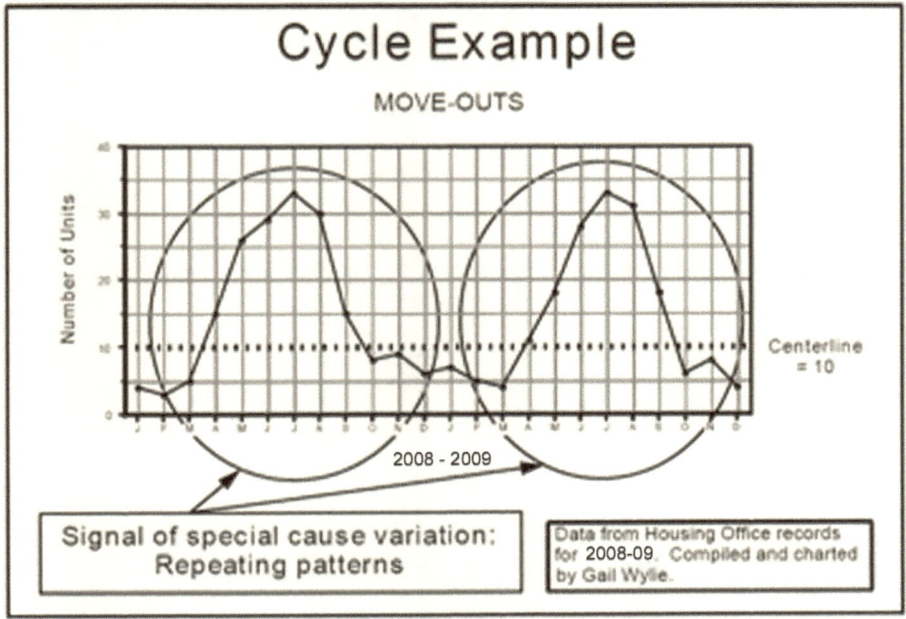

Figure 17: Run Chart: Cycle Example

Pareto Analysis

A Pareto Chart is "a series of bars whose heights reflect the frequency or impact of problems. The bars are arranged in descending order of height from left to right. This means the categories represented by the tall bars on the left are relatively more significant than those on the right" (Scholtes, 1989) The chart gets its name from the Pareto Principle, which postulates that 80 percent of the trouble comes from 20 percent of the problems.

Why Use a Pareto Chart?

➢ Breaks big problem into smaller pieces
➢ Identifies most significant factors
➢ Shows where to focus efforts
➢ Allows better use of limited resources

The Pareto Principle states that a small number of causes accounts for most of the problems. Focusing efforts on the 'vital few' causes is usually a better use of valuable resources". (*Basic Improvement Tools*. Madison, Instructor Guide)

When should we use a Pareto Chart?

A Pareto Chart is a good tool to use when the process you are investigating produces data that are broken down into categories and you can count the number of times each category occurs. No matter where you are in your process improvement efforts, Pareto Charts can be helpful, ". . . early on to identify which problem should be studied, later to narrow down which causes of the problem to address first. Since they draw everyone's attention to the 'vital few' important factors where the payback is likely to be greatest, (they) can be used to build consensus. In general, teams should focus their attention first on the biggest problems — those with the highest bars" (Scholtes, 1989) Making *problem-solving* decisions isn't the only use of the Pareto Principle. Since Pareto Charts convey information in a way that enables you to see clearly the choices that should be made, they can be used to *set priorities* for many practical applications in your company. Some examples are:

- Process improvement efforts for increased unit readiness
- Skills you want your division to have
- Customer needs
- Suppliers
- Investment opportunities

How is a Pareto Chart constructed?

To construct a Pareto Chart, you need to start with *meaningful* data which you have collected and categorized. You may want to turn to the Data Collection module at this point to review the process of collecting and categorizing data that you can chart. The steps below have been adapted from Joiner (*Basic Improvement Tools*. Madison, Workbook)

Constructing a Pareto Chart

Step 1 - Record the raw data. List each category and its associated data count.

Step 2 - Order the data. Prepare an analysis sheet, putting the categories in order and placing the one with the largest count first.

Step 3 - Label the left-hand vertical axis. Make sure the labels are spaced in equal intervals from 0 to a round number equal to or just larger than the total of all counts. Provide a caption to describe the unit of measurement being used.

Step 4 - Label the horizontal axis. Make the widths of all of the bars the same and label the categories from largest to smallest. An "other" category can be used last to capture several smaller sets of data. Provide a caption to describe them. If the contributor names are long, label the axis A, B, C, etc. and provide a key.

Step 5 - Plot a bar for each category. The height of each bar should equal the count for that category. The widths of the bars should be identical.

Step 6 - Find the cumulative counts. Each category's cumulative count is the count for that category added to the counts for all larger categories.

Step 7 - Add a cumulative line. This is optional. Label the right axis from 0 to 100%, and line up the 100% with the grand total on the left axis. For each category, put a dot as high as the cumulative total and in line with the right edge of that category's bar. Connect all the dots with straight lines.

Step 8 - Add title, legend, and date.

Step 9 - Analyze the diagram. Look for the break point on the cumulative percent graph. It can be identified by a marked change in the slope of the graph. This separates the significant few from the trivial many.

NOTE: *No matter how many data are categorized, they can be ranked and made into a Pareto diagram. The significant few-trivial many principle does not always hold.*

Now let's look at an example to illustrate the Pareto Chart construction process: *You recently inherited $10,000 and would like to apply it to some of your outstanding bills. Here is what you owe:*

Home improvement loan balance	$1,956
Visa	$2,007
Mastercard	$1,983
Church building fund pledge (monthly installments of $83.33 for two years)	$2,000
Balance of car loan	$1,971
School tuition (monthly installments of $169.17 for one year)	$2,030

Figures 18 and 19 show how this would look when recorded on an analysis sheet and plotted on a Pareto Chart.

Outstanding Debts

Category	Amount ($)
School tuition (monthly installments)	2,030
Visa	2,007
Church pledge (monthly installments)	2,000
Mastercard	1,983
Balance of car loan	1,971
Home improvement loan balance	1,956
Total	11,947

Figure 18 Analysis Sheet Example

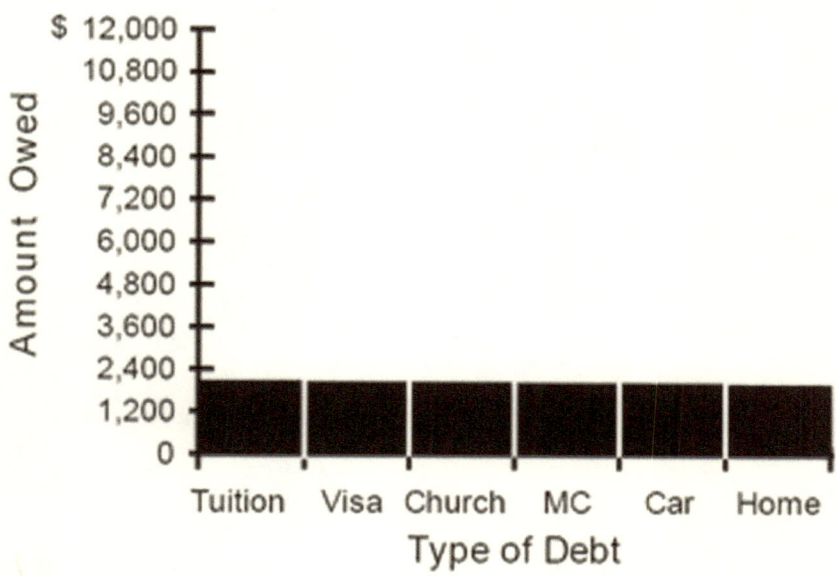

Outstanding Debts

LEGEND: AMOUNT OWED ON OUTSTANDING DEBTS

Figure 19 Pareto Chart Example

You probably noticed that no single bar is dramatically different from the others. Looking at your outstanding debts in this way isn't much help. Is there a different way the data could be categorized to make it more meaningful? What if you were to consider the interest rates on your outstanding debts? Figures 20 and 21 show what that would look like. A much clearer picture of your outstanding debts now emerges, and you are able to make a better decision on how to manage your money.

Interest Rates on Outstanding Debts

Category	Int. Rate (%)
Visa	21
Mastercard	18
Balance of car loan	9
Home improvement loan balance	6
School tuition (monthly installments)	2
Church pledge (monthly installments)	1

Figure 20 Analysis Sheet Example

Interest Rates on Outstanding Debts

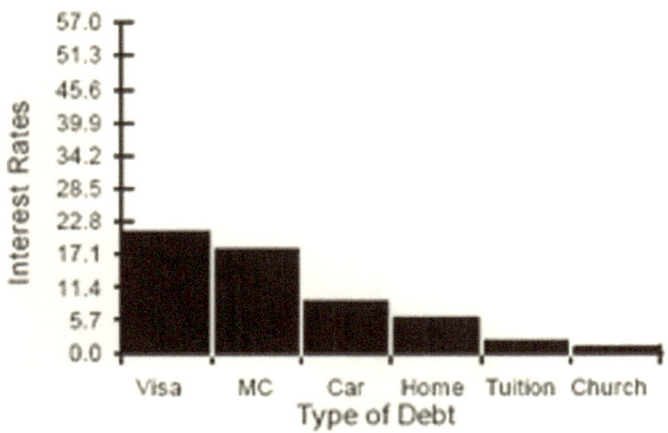

LEGEND: INTEREST RATES CHARGED ON OUTSTANDING DEBTS

Figure 21 Pareto Chart Example

NOTE: *In this example, we opted not to show a cumulative line (Step 7) on the right side of the Pareto Chart because it might be confusing to create a percentage of percentages.*

How do we interpret a Pareto Chart?

When you look at a Pareto Chart, you can see *break points* in the heights of the bars which indicate the most important categories. This information is useful when you are establishing priorities. As you can see in the example we've just looked at, (See Figure 21) you can detect two big breaks in the heights of the bars when you categorize the data in a different way:

- The first break point is between the second and third bars. The difference between these two bars is much more noticeable than the other differences. This shows the relative importance of the first two bars in relation to the others.
- The other break point occurs after the fourth bar. Addressing the third and fourth bars will give a higher payoff than addressing the last two bars.

"Perfection is not attainable. But if we chase perfection, we can catch excellence."

Vince Lombardi

Chapter 10: Putting SPC to Work

Control Charts

A control chart is a statistical tool used to distinguish between variation in a process resulting from common causes and variation resulting from special causes. It presents a graphic display of process stability or instability over time.

Every process has variation. Some variation may be the result of causes which are not normally present in the process. This could be *special cause variation*. Some variation is simply the result of numerous, ever-present differences in the process. This is *common cause variation*. Control Charts differentiate between these two types of variation. (See Figure 22 Process Variation)

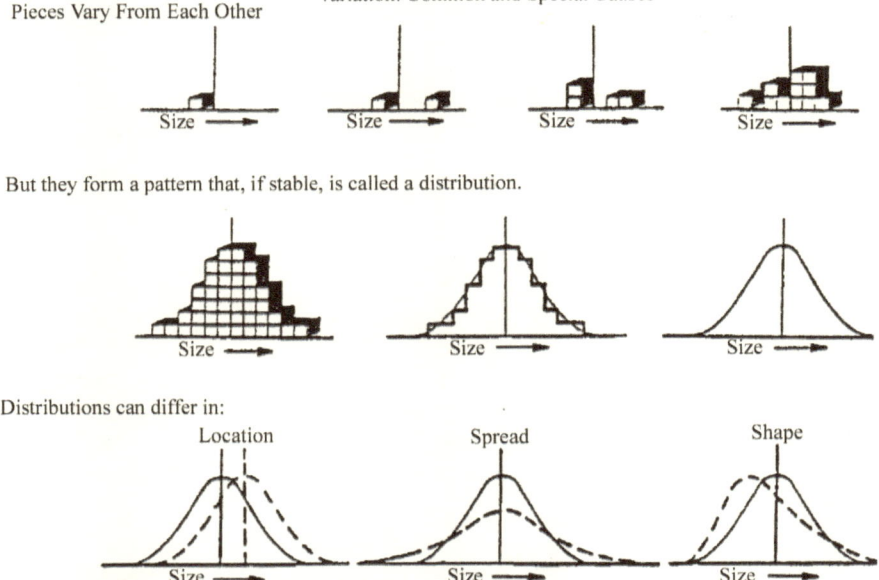

Figure 22 Process Variation

All variation in a product is caused by variation in one of the following: Material, Machines, Methods, Environment, and/or Operators.

One goal of using a Control Chart is to achieve and maintain *process stability*. Process stability is defined as a state in which a process has displayed a certain degree of consistency in the past and is expected to continue to do so in the future. This consistency is characterized by a stream of data falling within control limits based on plus or minus 3 standard deviations (3 sigma) of the centerline (Wheeler, D. J., & Chambers, D. S., 1992). We will discuss methods for calculating 3 sigma limits later in this chapter.

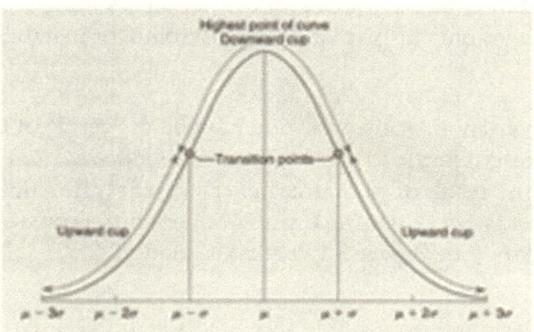

The area under the curve is represented by +/- 1 to 3 standard deviations from the center:

$\mu \pm 1\sigma$	68.26% under the curve (31.74% outside the curve)
$\mu \pm 2\sigma$	95.46% under the curve (04.54% outside the curve)
$\mu \pm 3\sigma$	99.73% under the curve (00.27% outside the curve)

Three sigma quality means there are .27% defects. (i.e. about 1 defect out of 300)

Figure 23 Three Sigma Quality

NOTE: *Control limits represent the limits of variation that should be expected from a process in a state of statistical control. When a process is in statistical control, any variation is the result of common causes that effect the entire production in a similar way. Control limits should not be confused with specification limits, which represent the desired process performance.*

What does variation have to do with process capability?

If only common causes of variation are present, the output of the process forms a distribution that is stable and predictable over time. Recall common causes of variation are the result of numerous, ever-present differences in the process. (See Figure 24 Stable Process)

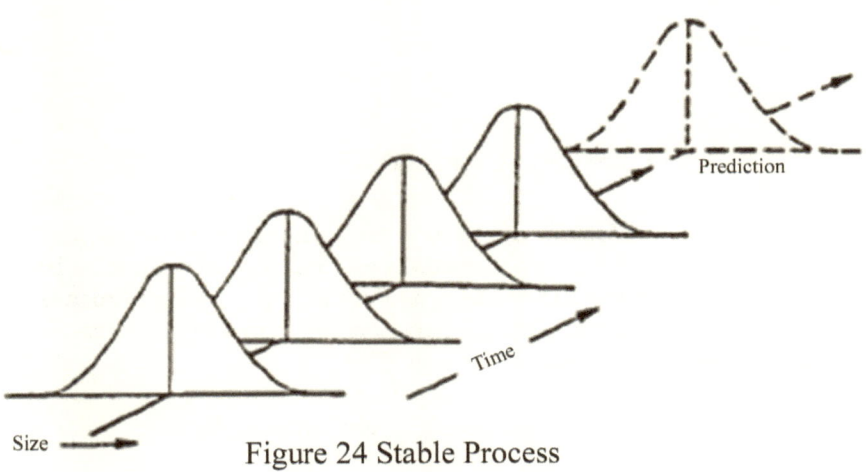

Figure 24 Stable Process

Next we see a process that is in control, but not capable, due to excessive variation in common causes. The tails of the distribution extend beyond the upper and lower specifications, yet the pattern still forms a "normal distribution". We may see this often as a company first begins to use Statistical Process Control (SPC) techniques.

In this instance, our first goal must be to identify and remove as many of the common causes of the variation as possible. (See Figure 25 In Control But Not Capable)

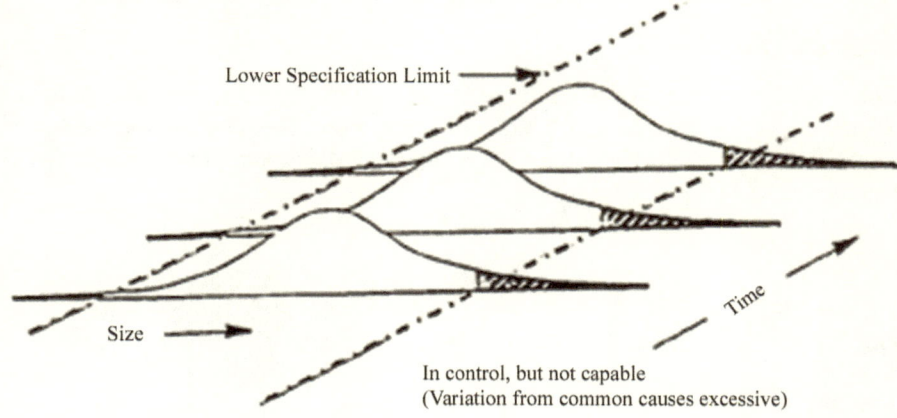

Lower Specification Limit

Size

Time

In control, but not capable
(Variation from common causes excessive)

Figure 25 In Control But Not Capable

The extent of common causes of variation can be indicated by simple statistical techniques; however, the causes themselves may be more difficult to isolate. Common causes of variation are usually under the responsibility of management to correct. Often operators are in a better position to identify these causes and pass them on to management.

Note: *The resolution of common causes usually requires actions on the system.*

Only a relatively small portion of all process troubles is correctable locally by the operators. Deming says 94% of all problems are directly under the control of management and only 6% are under the control of the operators.

The bottom line is, simply telling the front line employees things like be careful, watch what they are doing, and don't make mistakes, will do little to actually improve process capability or the quality of the product. It will, in fact, increase the employees' frustration and potentially *make them even less likely to do their best!*

Special causes of variation can be detected by simple statistical techniques. These causes of variation are not common to all the operations involved. The discovery of a special cause of variation, and its removal, is usually the responsibility of someone that is directly connected with the operation. The resolution of a special cause of variation usually requires local action. In other words, this is usually directly under the control of the front line employee.

Figure 26 illustrates a process that is out of control because of a special cause. A special cause is a source variation that is intermittent, unpredictable, and unstable. (On a control chart it would be represented by a point beyond the control limits or a nonrandom series of points within control limits.)

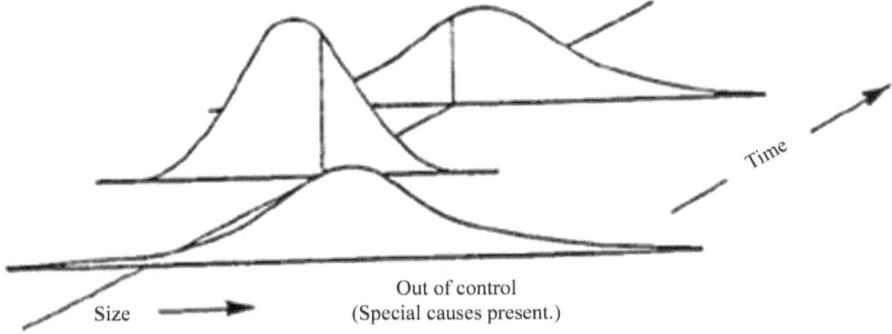

Figure 26 Out of Control due to Special Cause

The process must first be brought into statistical control by detecting and eliminating special causes of variation. Then its performance is predictable and its capability to meet customer expectations can be assessed. This is the basis for continuing improvement.

Why should teams use Control Charts?

A stable process is one that is consistent over time with respect to the center and the spread of the data. Control Charts help you monitor the behavior of your process to determine whether it is stable. Like Run Charts, they display data in the time sequence in which they occurred. However, Control Charts are more efficient than Run Charts in assessing and achieving process stability. Your team will benefit from using a Control Chart when you want to:

➤ Monitor process variation over time.

➤ Differentiate between special cause and common cause variation.

➤ Assess the effectiveness of changes to improve a process.

➤ Communicate how a process performed during a specific period.

A control chart is nothing more than a series of distributions with the upper and lower control limits representing boundaries beyond which the tails of the distribution should not extend.

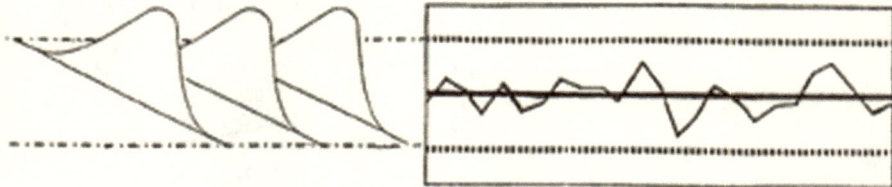

Figure 27 Control Chart Concept

Each point on the control chart actually represents the average value of an individual distribution. In other words, let's say we are taking 5 consecutive samples of our product every 30 minutes. Taken individually, we would have a distribution as illustrated in Figure 22. In order to represent this information on a control chart, we would average the data and determine a single value for those 5 samples. The new value is then plotted (as a single point) on a control chart for that specific time period.

The figure shown below represents a typical control chart with both the upper and lower control limits identified, the upper and lower specifications noted, as well as the process average. The specification limits would not necessarily be evenly spaced as illustrated.

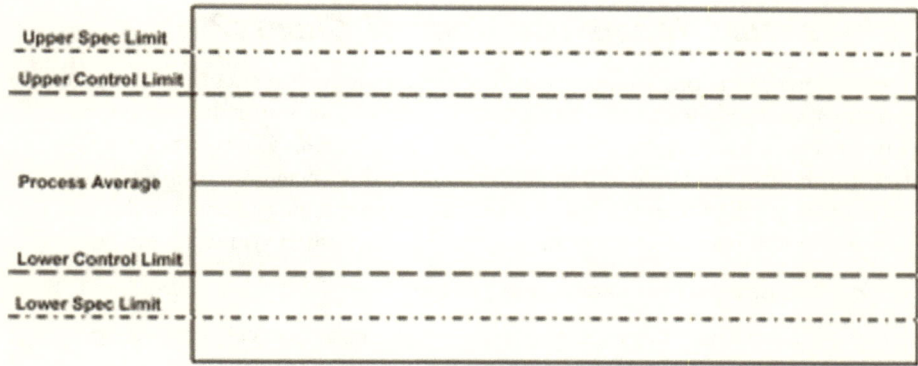

Figure 28 Typical Control Chart

The manufacturing process talks to us; however, we usually don't listen. In most cases, the process will tell us *before it begins to make defective products*. Control Charts let us listen to the process and allow us to make adjustments as necessary (and only when necessary) to the equipment preventing defective products from being made.

In Figure 29a, we see a process that has been stable and in control; however, when we plotted our last series of observations, we noted a single data point is above the Upper Control Limit. (Recall, that single data point actually represents the average value of a sample of observations.) This is now an out of control situation. But, since we have not gone outside of our upper specification limit, we have not yet made a defective product. *The process is talking to us, telling us that something is going wrong!*

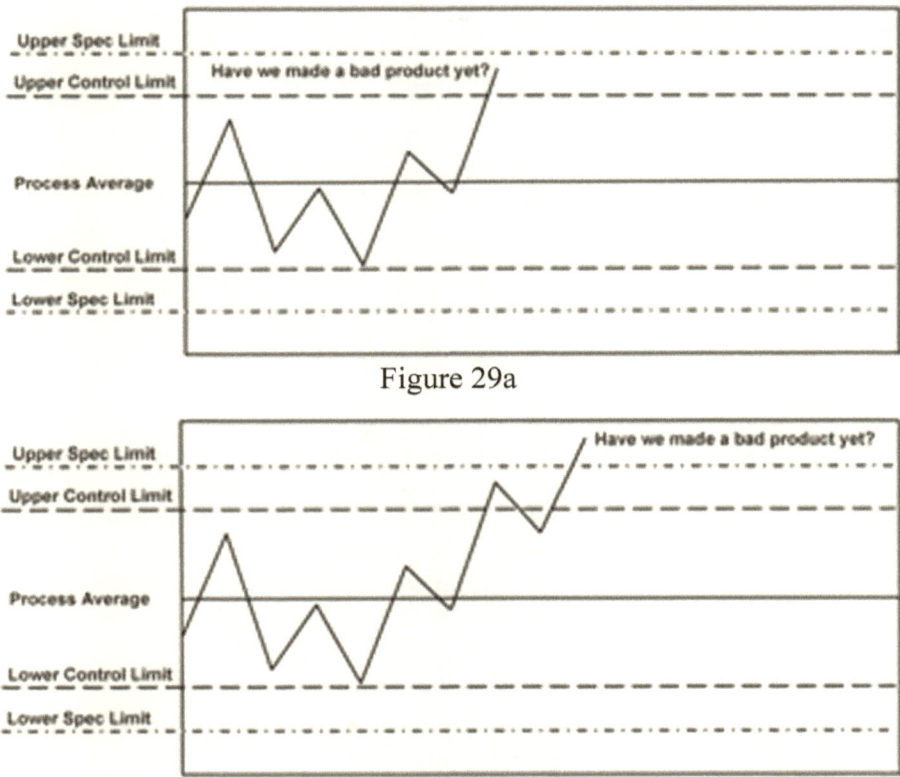

Figure 29a

Figure 29b

If no action is taken, we might very well find ourselves in the situation illustrated in Figure 29b. At a specified time another set of data was collected and the point was below the control limit. However, since no action was taken to discover and eliminate the special cause of the variation, we now have an out of control situation and *we are now producing defective products!*

What happens when a process is in control but not capable?

Recall Figure 25, this process is in control, but not capable, due to excessive variation in common causes. The tails of the distribution extend beyond the upper and lower specifications, yet the pattern still forms a "normal distribution". A process that is in control, but not capable, is illustrated by the control chart shown in Figure 30. Remember, this process is not capable because of excessive process variation due to common causes.

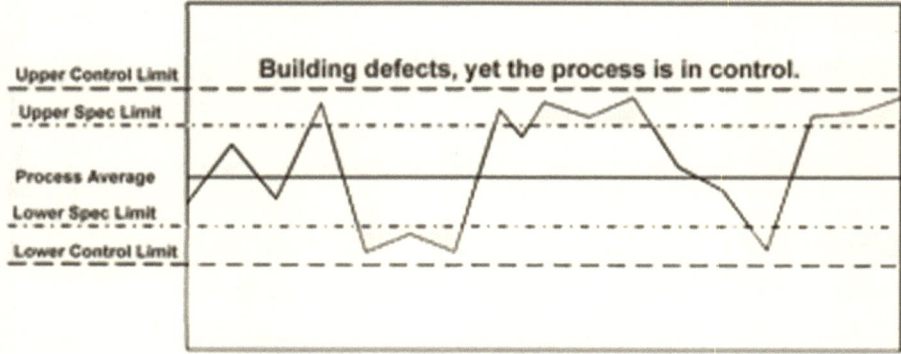

Figure 30 In Control Building Defects

In this situation, there is little, if anything, an operator can do to prevent the machine from building defective product. In fact, machine operators often cause more problems when they yield to the temptation to make adjustments to the equipment in order to reduce the defects produced. Tinkering or attempting to fine tune a process that is in control (even if is not capable) will just cause more problems. This situation is often discovered when a company first begins to implement SPC techniques.

What are the types of Control Charts?

There are two main categories of Control Charts, those that display *attribute data*, and those that display *variables data*.

Attribute Data: This category of Control Chart displays data that result from counting the number of occurrences or items in a single category of similar items or occurrences. These "count" data may be expressed as pass/fail, yes/no, or presence/absence of a defect.

Variables Data: This category of Control Chart displays values resulting from the measurement of a continuous variable. Examples of variables data are elapsed time, temperature, and radiation dose.

While these two categories encompass a number of different types of Control Charts there are several types that will work for the majority of the data analysis cases you will encounter. In this chapter, we will focus on the construction and application of the X-Bar and R Charts:

➢ Individual X-Bar and Range Chart for Variables Data
➢ Individual X-Bar and Range Chart for Attribute Data

What are the elements of a Control Chart?

Each Control Chart actually consists of *two graphs*, an upper and a lower, which are described below under *plotting areas*. A Control Chart is made up of eight elements. The first three are identified in Figure 31; the other five in Figure 32.

1. Title. The title briefly describes the information which is displayed.

2. Legend. This is information on how and when the data were collected.

3. Data Collection Section. The counts or measurements are recorded in the data collection section of the Control Chart prior to being graphed.

4. Plotting Areas. A Control Chart has two areas — an upper graph and a lower graph — where the data is plotted.

> a. The upper graph plots either the individual values, in the case of an Individual X and Moving Range chart, or the average (mean value) of the sample or subgroup in the case of an X-Bar and R chart.

> b. The lower graph plots the moving range for Individual X and Moving Range charts, or the range of values found in the subgroups for X-Bar and R charts.

5. Vertical or Y-Axis. This axis reflects the magnitude of the data collected. The Y-axis shows the scale of the measurement for *variables data*, or the count (frequency) or percentage of occurrence of an event for *attribute data*.

6. Horizontal or X-Axis. This axis displays the chronological order in which the data were collected.

7. Control Limits. Control limits are set at a distance of 3 sigma above and sigma below the centerline. (Wheeler, D. J., & Chambers, D. S., 1992) They indicate variation from the centerline and are calculated by using the actual values plotted on the Control Chart graphs.

8. Centerline. This line is drawn at the average or mean value of all the plotted data. The upper and lower graphs each have a separate centerline.

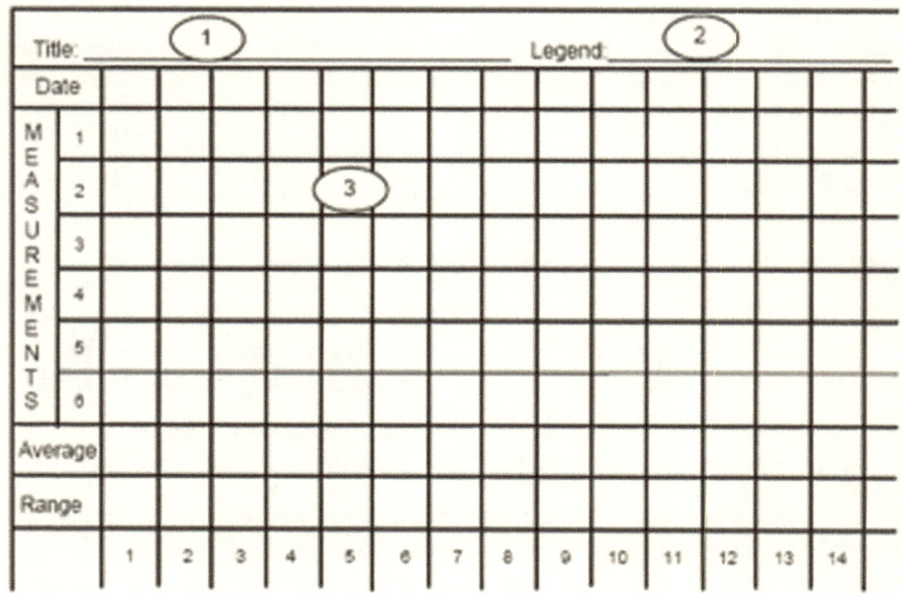

Figure 31 Control Chart Information Collection

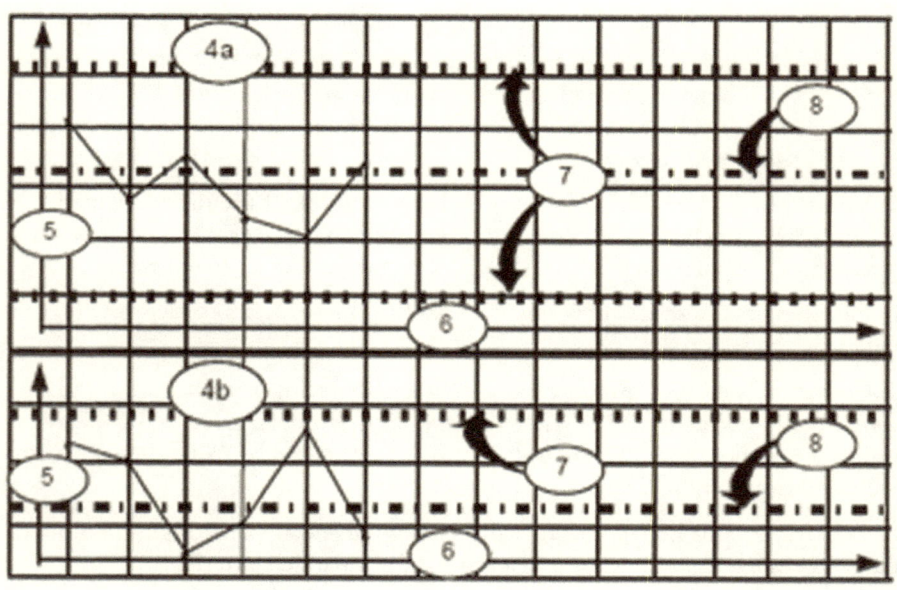

Figure 32 Control Chart Plotting Area

What are the steps for calculating and plotting an X-Bar and R Control Chart for Variables Data?

The X-Bar (arithmetic mean) and R (range) Control Chart is used with variables data when subgroup or sample size is between 2 and 15. The steps for constructing this type of Control Chart are:

Step 1 - Determine the data to be collected. Decide what questions about the process you plan to answer. Refer to the Chapter 8, Data Collection, for information on how this is done.

Step 2 - Collect and enter the data by subgroup. A subgroup is made up of variables data that represent a characteristic of a product produced by a process. The *sample size* relates to how large the subgroups are. Enter the individual subgroup measurements in time sequence in the portion of the data collection section of the Control Chart labeled *Measurements* (Figure 33).

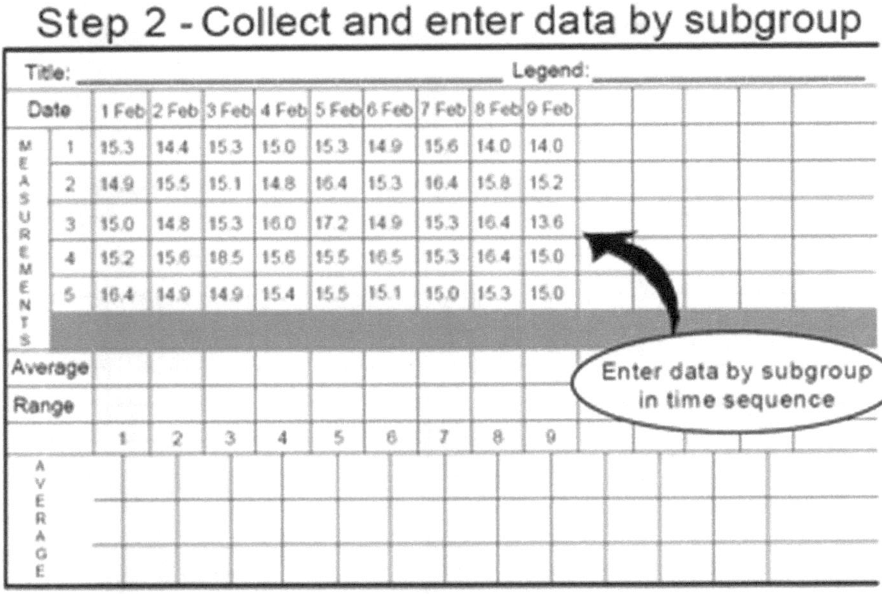

Step 2 - Collect and enter data by subgroup

Title: _____ Legend: _____

Date		1 Feb	2 Feb	3 Feb	4 Feb	5 Feb	6 Feb	7 Feb	8 Feb	9 Feb					
M E A S U R E M E N T S	1	15.3	14.4	15.3	15.0	15.3	14.9	15.6	14.0	14.0					
	2	14.9	15.5	15.1	14.8	16.4	15.3	16.4	15.8	15.2					
	3	15.0	14.8	15.3	16.0	17.2	14.9	15.3	16.4	13.6					
	4	15.2	15.6	18.5	15.6	15.5	16.5	15.3	16.4	15.0					
	5	16.4	14.9	14.9	15.4	15.5	15.1	15.0	15.3	15.0					
Average															
Range															
		1	2	3	4	5	6	7	8	9					

Enter data by subgroup in time sequence

Figure 33 Collect and enter the data by subgroup

STEP 3 - Calculate and enter the average for each subgroup. Use the formula below to calculate the average (mean) for each subgroup and enter it on the line labeled *Average* in the data collection section (Figure 34).

$$\overline{X} = \frac{X_1 + X_2 + X_3 + \ldots X_n}{n}$$

Where: $\overline{X}$ = The average of the measurements within each subgroup
x_i = The individual measurements within a subgroup
n = The number of measurements within a subgroup

Average Example

Subgroup	1	2	3	4	5	6	7	8	9
X_1	15.3	14.4	15.3	15.0	15.3	14.9	15.6	14.0	14.0
X_2	14.9	15.5	15.1	14.8	16.4	15.3	16.4	15.8	15.2
X_3	15.0	14.8	15.3	16.0	17.2	14.9	15.3	16.4	13.6
X_4	15.2	15.6	18.5	15.6	15.5	16.5	15.3	16.4	15.0
X_5	16.4	14.9	14.9	15.4	15.5	15.1	15.0	15.3	15.0
Average:	15.36	15.04	15.82	15.36	15.98	15.34	15.52	15.58	14.56

$$\overline{X} = \frac{15.3 + 14.9 + 15.0 + 15.2 + 16.4}{5} = \frac{76.8}{5} = 15.36$$

Step 3 - Calculate and enter subgroup averages

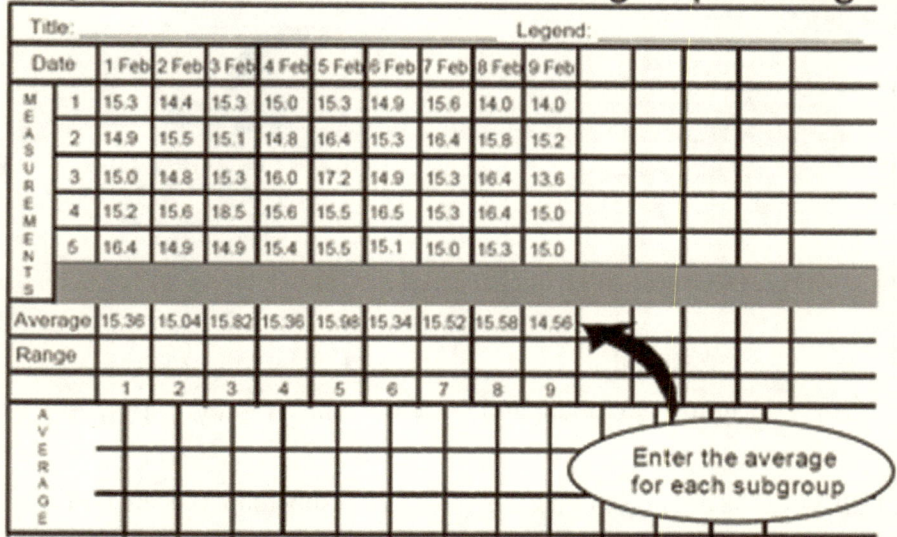

Figure 34 Enter Averages

Step 4 - Calculate and enter the range for each subgroup. Use the following formula to calculate the range (R) for each subgroup. Enter the range for each subgroup on the line labeled *Range* in the data collection section (Figure 35).

RANGE = (Largest Value in each Subgroup) − (Smallest Value in each Subgroup)

Range Example

Subgroup	1	2	3	4	5	6	7	8	9
X_1	15.3	14.4	15.3	15.0	15.3	14.9	15.6	14.0	14.0
X_2	14.9	15.5	15.1	14.8	16.4	15.3	16.4	15.8	15.2
X_3	15.0	14.8	15.3	16.0	17.2	14.9	15.3	16.4	13.6
X_4	15.2	15.6	18.5	15.6	15.5	16.5	15.3	16.4	15.0
X_5	16.4	14.9	14.9	15.4	15.5	15.1	15.0	15.3	15.0
Average:	15.36	15.04	15.82	15.36	15.98	15.34	15.52	15.58	14.56
Range:	1.5	1.2	3.6	1.2	1.9	1.6	1.4	2.4	1.6

Step 4 - Calculate and enter subgroup ranges

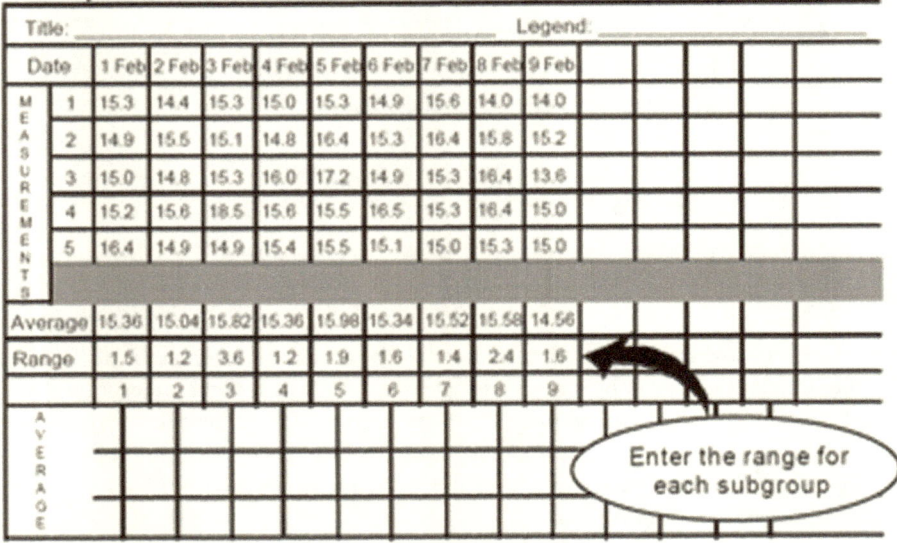

Figure 35 Enter the Range

Step 5 - Calculate the *grand mean* of the subgroup's average. The *grand mean* of the subgroup's average (X-Bar) becomes the centerline for the upper plot.

$$\overline{\overline{x}} = \frac{\overline{X_1} + \overline{X_2} + \overline{X_3} + \ldots \overline{X_k}}{k}$$

Where: $\overline{\overline{x}}$ = The grand mean of all the individual subgroup averages
$\overline{x}$ = The average for each subgroup
k = The number of subgroups

Grand Mean Example

$$\overline{\overline{x}} = \frac{15.36 + 15.04 + 15.82 + 15.36 + 15.98 + 15.34 + 15.52 + 15.58 + 14.56}{9} = \frac{138.56}{9} = 15.40$$

Step 6 - Calculate the average of the subgroup ranges. The average of all subgroups becomes the centerline for the lower plotting area.

$$\overline{R} = \frac{R_1 + R_2 + R_3 + \ldots R_k}{k}$$

Where: R_i = The individual range for each subgroup
$\overline{R}$ = The average of the ranges for all subgroups
k = The number of subgroups

Average of Ranges Example

$$\overline{R} = \frac{1.5 + 1.2 + 3.6 + 1.2 + 1.9 + 1.6 + 1.4 + 2.4 + 1.6}{9} = \frac{16.4}{9} = 1.8$$

Step 7 - Calculate the upper control limit (UCL) and lower control limit (LCL) for the averages of the subgroups. At this point, your chart will look like a Run Chart. Now, however, the uniqueness of the Control Chart becomes evident as you calculate the control limits. Control limits define the parameters for determining whether a process is in statistical control. To find the X-Bar control limits, use the following formula:

$$UCL_{\overline{x}} = \overline{\overline{X}} + A_2\overline{R}$$
$$LCL_{\overline{x}} = \overline{\overline{X}} - A_2\overline{R}$$

NOTE: *Constants, based on the subgroup size (n), are used in determining control limits for variables charts. Use the following constants (A2) in the computation.*

You can learn more about constants in *Tools and Methods for the Improvement of Quality* (Gitlow, H., Gitlow, S., Oppenheim, A., Oppenheim, R., 1989)

Use the following constants (A_2) in the computation

n	A_2	n	A_2	n	A_2
2	1.880	7	0.419	12	0.266
3	1.023	8	0.373	13	0.249
4	0.729	9	0.337	14	0.235
5	0.577	10	0.308	15	0.223
6	0.483	11	0.285		

Step 8 - Calculate the upper control limit for the ranges. When the subgroup or sample size (n) is less than 7, there is no lower control limit. To find the upper control limit for the ranges, use the formula: $UCL_R = D_4 \overline{R}$

$LCL_R = D_3 \overline{R}$ (for subgroups $\geq$ 7)

Upper and Lower Control Limits Example

$$UCL_{\overline{X}} = \overline{\overline{X}} + A_2 \overline{R} = (15.40) + (0.577)(1.8) = 16.4386$$
$$LCL_{\overline{X}} = \overline{\overline{X}} - A_2 \overline{R} = (15.40) - (0.577)(1.8) = 14.3614$$

Use the following constants (D_4) in the computation

n	D_4	n	D_4	n	D_4
2	3.267	7	1.924	12	1.717
3	2.574	8	1.864	13	1.693
4	2.282	9	1.816	14	1.672
5	2.114	10	1.777	15	1.653
6	2.004	11	1.744		

Example

$$UCL_R = D_4 \overline{R} = (2.114)(1.8) = 3.8052$$

Step 9 - Select the scales and plot the control limits, centerline, and data points, in each plotting area. The scales must be determined before the data points and centerline can be plotted. Once the upper and lower control limits have been computed, the easiest way to select the scales is to have the current data take up approximately 60 percent of the vertical (Y) axis. The scales for both the upper and lower plotting areas should allow for future high or low out of control data points.

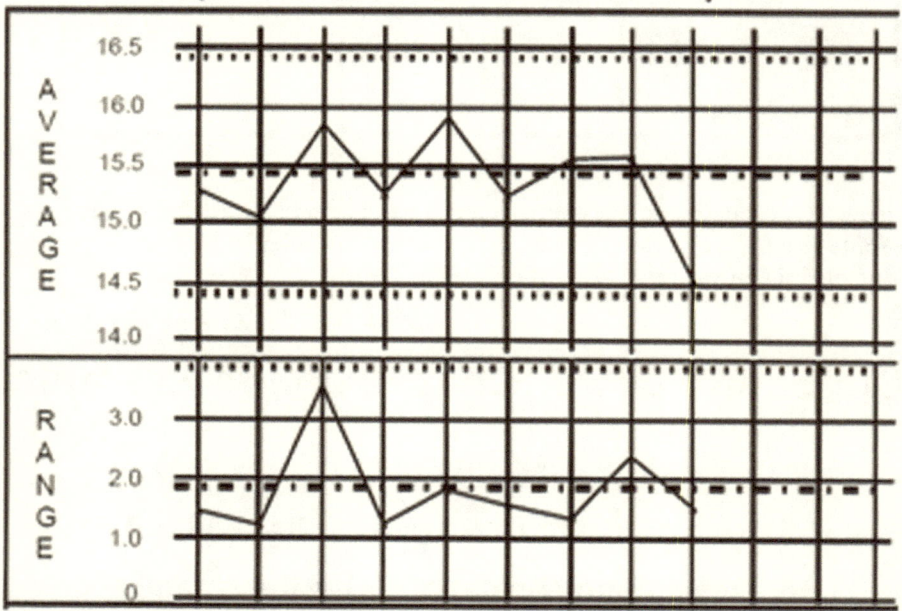

Figure 36 Select the scales and plot

Plot each subgroup average as an individual data point in the upper plotting area. Plot individual range data points in the lower plotting area (Figure 36).

Step 10 - Provide the appropriate documentation. Each Control Chart should be labeled with who, what, when, where, why, and how information to describe where the data originated, when it was collected, who collected it, any identifiable equipment or work groups, sample size, and all the other things necessary for understanding and interpreting it. It is important that the legend include all of the information that clarifies what the data describe.

What do we need to know to interpret Control Charts?

Process stability is reflected in the relatively constant variation exhibited in Control Charts. Basically, the data fall within a band bounded by the control limits. If a process is stable, the likelihood of a point falling outside this band is so small that such an occurrence is taken as a signal of a special cause of variation. In other words, something abnormal is occurring within your process. However, even though all the points fall inside the control limits, special cause variation may be at work. The presence of unusual patterns can be evidence that your process is not in statistical control. Such patterns are more likely to occur when one or more special causes are present.

Control Charts are based on control limits which are 3 standard deviations (3 sigma) away from the centerline. You should resist the urge to narrow these limits in the hope of identifying special causes earlier. Experience has shown that limits based on less than plus and minus 3 sigma may lead to false assumptions about special causes operating in a process. (Wheeler, D. J., & Chambers, D. S., 1992) In other words, using control limits that are less than 3 sigma from the centerline may trigger a hunt for special causes when the process is already stable.

The three standard deviations are sometimes identified by zones. Each zone's dividing line is exactly one-third the distance from the centerline to either the upper control limit or the lower control limit (Figure 37).

> ➢ Zone A is defined as the area between 2 and 3 standard deviations from the centerline on both the plus and minus sides of the centerline.

> ➢ Zone B is defined as the area between 1 and 2 standard deviations from the centerline on both sides of the centerline.

> ➢ Zone C is defined as the area between the centerline and 1 standard deviation from the centerline, on both sides of the centerline.

NOTE: *These rules should not be confused with the rules for interpreting Run Charts.*

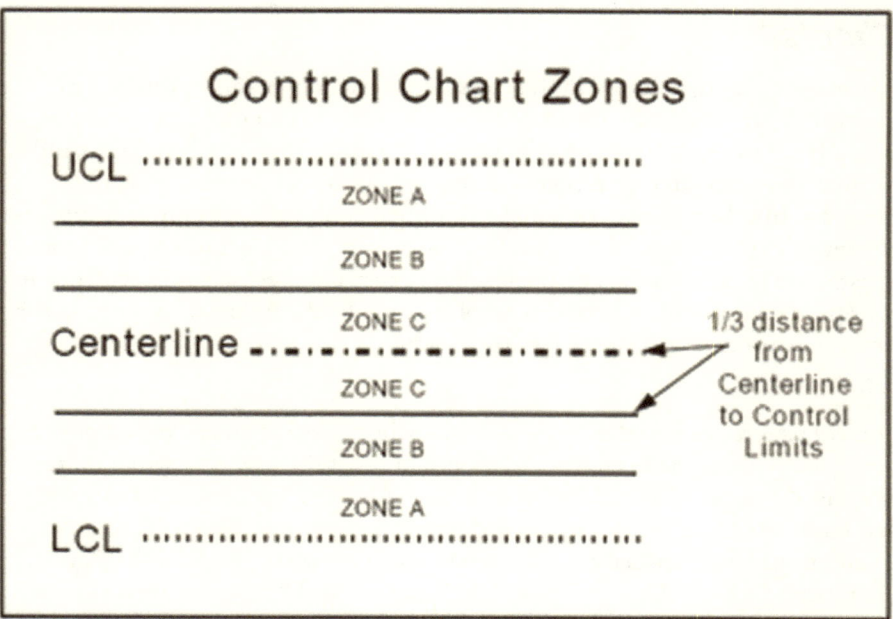

Figure 37 Control Chart Zones

What are the rules for interpreting X-Bar and R Charts?

When a special cause is affecting the data, the nonrandom patterns displayed in a Control Chart will be fairly obvious. The key to these rules is recognizing that they serve as a signal for when to investigate what occurred in the process. When you are interpreting X-Bar and R Control Charts, you should apply the following set of rules:

RULE 1: (Figure 38): Whenever a single point falls outside the 3 sigma control limits, a lack of control is indicated. Since the probability of this happening is rather small, it is very likely not due to chance.

RULE 2: (Figure 39): Whenever at least 2 out of 3 successive values fall on the same side of the centerline and more than 2 sigma units away from the centerline (in Zone A or beyond), a lack of control is indicated. Note that the third point can be on either side of the centerline.

RULE 3: (Figure 40): Whenever at least 4 out of 5 successive values fall on the same side of the centerline and more than one sigma unit away from the centerline (in Zones A or B or beyond), a lack of control is indicated. Note that the fifth point can be on either side of the centerline.

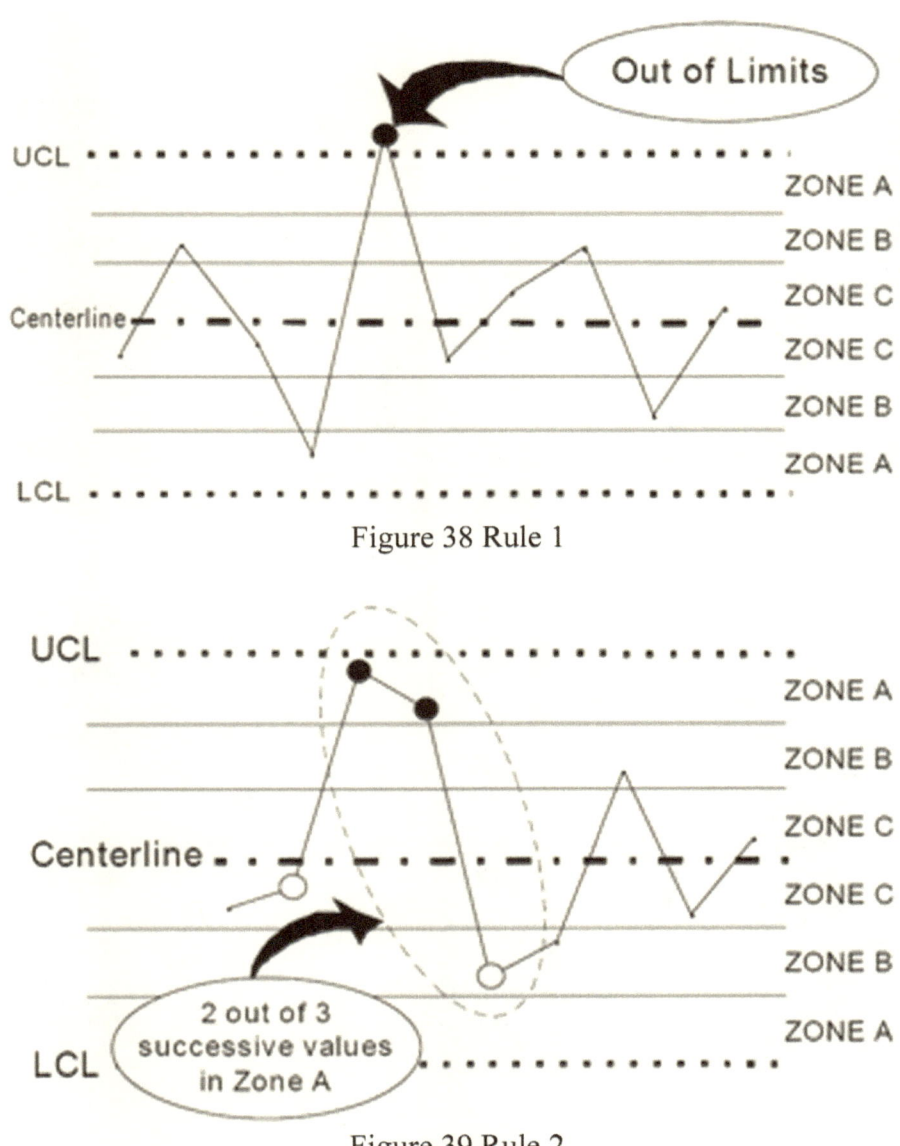

Figure 38 Rule 1

Figure 39 Rule 2

RULE 4: (Figure 41): Whenever at least 8 successive values fall on the same side of the centerline, a lack of control is indicated.

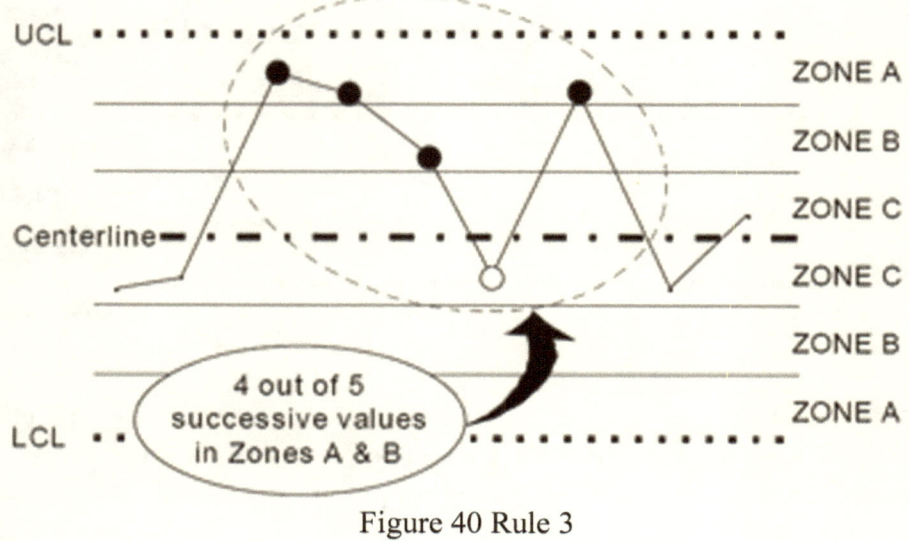

Figure 40 Rule 3

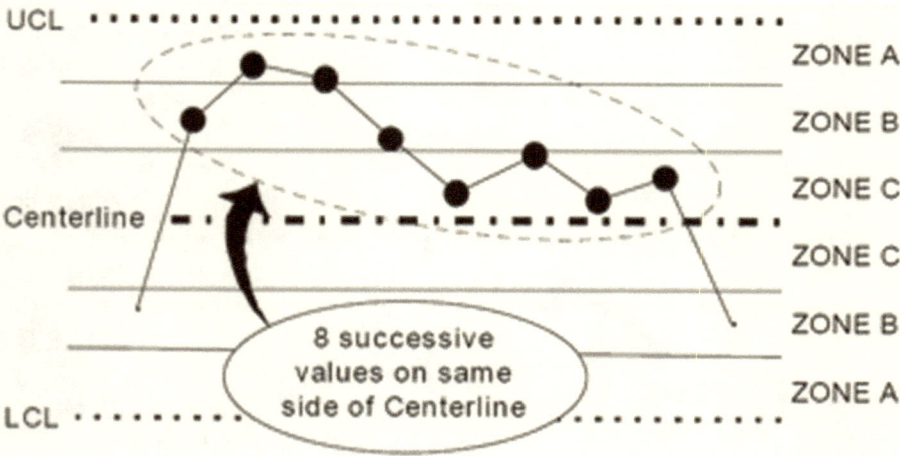

Figure 41 Rule 4

RULE 5: (Figure 42) In this chart, since there is a long run that is very close to the centerline, we see a situation that is also out of control; however, this is not necessarily bad! This chart indicates that the process has changed (meaning out of control), but this time we are actually making a product that may be better than before since there is less variation than we would normally expects to see. We want to determine what has changed and make it a permanent part of the process.

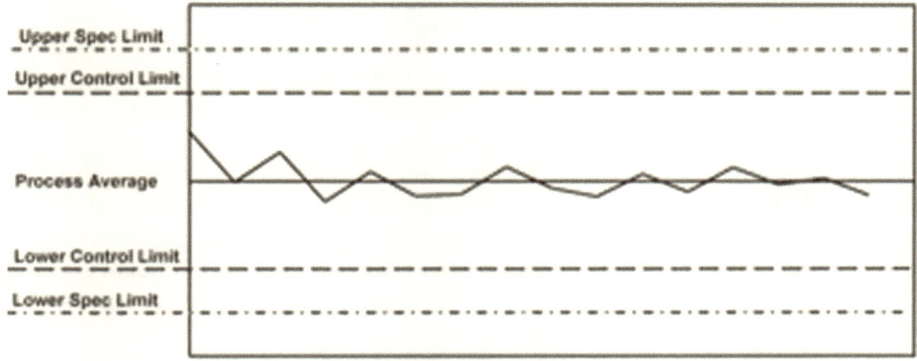

Figure 42 Rule 5

When should we change the control limits?

There are only three situations in which it is appropriate to change the control limits:

➢ When removing out of control data points. When a special cause has been identified and removed while you are working to achieve process stability, you may want to delete the data points affected by special causes and use the remaining data to compute new control limits.

➢ When replacing trial limits. When a process has just started up, or has changed, you may want to calculate control limits using only the limited data available. These limits are usually called *trial control limits*. You can calculate new limits every time you add new data. Once you have 20 or 30 groups of 4 or 5 measurements without a signal, you can use the limits to monitor future performance. You don't need to recalculate the limits again unless fundamental changes are made to the process.

➢ When there are changes in the process. When there are indications that your process has changed, it is necessary to recompute the control limits based on data collected since the change occurred. Some examples of such changes are the application of new or modified procedures, the use of different machines, the overhaul of existing machines, and the introduction of new suppliers of critical input materials.

What is Six Sigma Quality?

Recall when talking about three sigma quality we were essentially measuring our defect rate in parts per hundred. (See Figure 23) When our process is in control and we have achieved a three sigma level of quality, then 99.73% of our product is acceptable and .27% is defective. This equates to about one defect in three hundred or 1350 defects per million defect opportunities. Six Sigma quality means that we are now looking plus or minus 6 standard deviations from the center of the normal distribution! This equates to .001 defects per million defect opportunities. (Figure 43) Motorola was among the first to strive for Six Sigma Quality.

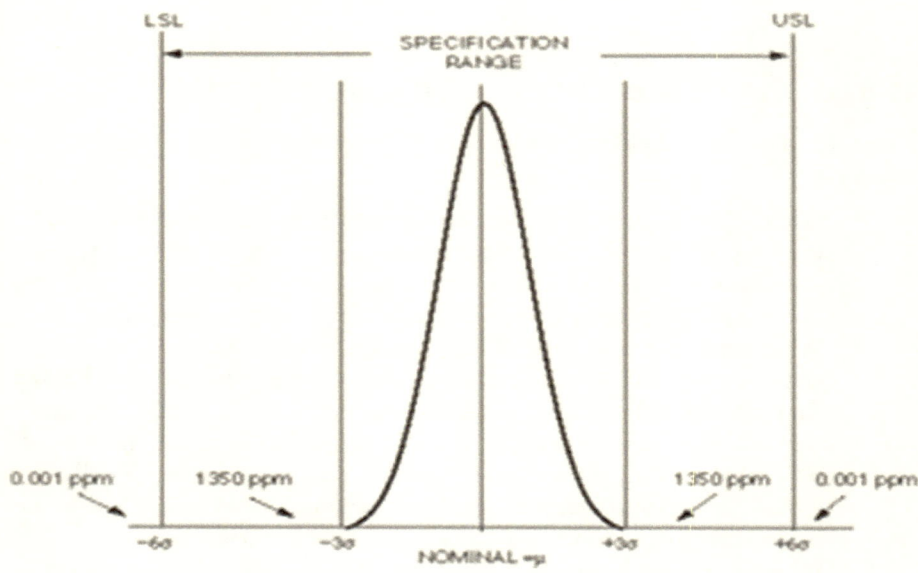

Figure 43 Six Sigma Quality

"Success is the ability to go from one failure to another with no loss of enthusiasm."

Sir Winston Churchill

Chapter 11: Thinking Lean

What does it mean to have a Lean Culture?

The concept of Lean Manufacturing has it roots in what is known as the Toyota Production System. The Allied victory and the massive quantities of material behind it caught the attention of Japanese industrialists and the Toyota Motor Company in particular. For many years they studied American production methods with particular attention to Ford's mass production techniques and the Statistical Quality Control practices of Ishikawa, W. Edwards Deming, and Joseph Juran. They also studied, of all things, our American supermarkets!

Taiichi Ohno and Shigeo Shingo developed and implemented Toyota Production System over a period of 20-30 years. Their approach provides a model for other implementations and has become known as Lean Manufacturing.

Ohno   **Shingo**

Ohno first visualized an ideal production system, in terms of workflow. Ohno's ideal system was inspired Eiji Toyoda's observations at Ford Motor Company. Henry Ford wrote in 1922, "We have found in buying materials that it is not worthwhile to buy for other than immediate needs." He went on to say, "We buy only enough to fit into the plan of production, taking into consideration the state of transportation at the time." Ohno believed the ideal production system was a series of adjacent workstations that were balanced and synchronized with no inventory between stations. It delivered finished product to the customer exactly when needed (Just-In-Time) and drew materials, just-in-time.

According to legend, Ohno asked Shingo and others what prevented the realization of this ultimate, no-inventory system. As the reasons surfaced, Ohno requested his deputies to "eliminate the reasons."

The resulting elements of Lean Manufacturing aim at eliminating (or at least reducing) the reasons for inventory. *While the real goal is to eliminate waste, Ohno understood that inventory mirrors waste.*

This is an example of what Edward DeBono calls "Lateral Thinking." By imagining an ideal, but impossible situation, we can often see more clearly, the path to its realization.

Ohno and Shingo did not intend to develop some sort of "Unified Field Theory" for all manufacturing. They simply wanted to solve Toyota's specific problems. The solutions they chose, while broad based, do not necessarily apply in all situations. Your solutions may be different.

In many factories, a primary "reason for inventory" involves intertwined issues of equipment scale, setup, batching, and workflow. The causal diagram (Figure 44) illustrates.

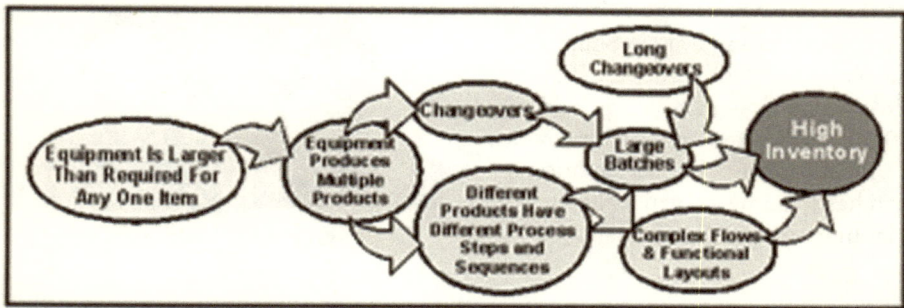

Figure 44 Cause of High Inventory

The problem starts with equipment that is larger and faster than required for a single product. This causes multiple products to run on the same equipment. Two effects ensue:

    1) Changeovers become necessary.

    2) Different products follow different routes.

In addition, large-scale equipment often requires difficult and time-consuming setups. The combination of changeover and long setup forces large batches that promote high inventory. Different routes force functional layouts with complex flows that also increase inventory.

High inventory brings all sorts of waste in material handling, space, and quality. This illustration is over-simplified. In reality, it has multiple, subtle reinforcing loops that exacerbate the problem over time.

At Toyota, Shingo attacked both root causes. First, he developed the Single Minute Exchange of Die (SMED) system that reduced changeover times and, thus, batch sizes and inventory. Second, *he scaled down the equipment*, where possible, thus enabling Cellular Manufacturing and its simplified workflow.

SMED and workcells did not become part of the Toyota Production System because they had some sort of cosmic virtue. They were employed because they reduced inventory and waste in the Toyota context.

The model is simple; the implications profound. It led Toyota to setup reduction, workcells and, eventually, the other tools of Lean Manufacturing. In other situations, it may lead to a somewhat different set of tools. The moral is:

➢ Do not copy Toyota's tools and techniques; they are not universal.

➢ Use Toyota's model it is universal.

The Lean Manufacturing background information is courtesy of Strategos, Inc., for more information please visit www.strategosinc.com.

Eliminate what kind of waste?

There are seven forms of waste that can be found in business.

1. Correction – Anytime you have to go back and correct mistakes or repair defective product. Typically, the costs here as almost three time the original cost to manufacture.

2. Overproduction – Producing to much WIP by letting equipment run full speed and then holding excessive amounts of parts in inventory until needed - sometimes months later!

3. Material Movement – Here is a classic example of waste in a typical manufacturing plant. Parts come off a line and are hand packed into crates. The crates are moved by forklift to packaging where the crates are wrapped in plastic for outside storage. At some point – weeks or months later, the crates are moved again to the loading dock. From the dock they are moved again to an inspection area where the crates are unwrapped and parts are individually cleaned and inspected. Finally, the parts are moved to the manufacturing area and used.

4. Motion – This is the individual's motion. Be on the lookout for wasted hand motions and extra steps.

5. Waiting – Needless to say, if you are waiting on parts, that's a waste.

6. Inventory – Holding excessive inventory, of any kind, is a waste.

7. Over Processing – Doing additional things to a part that does not impact on the fit, form, or function. Taking a file and de-burring a pipe when the rough edge is going to be covered by a cap is an example of "Over Processing".

Lean Manufacturing

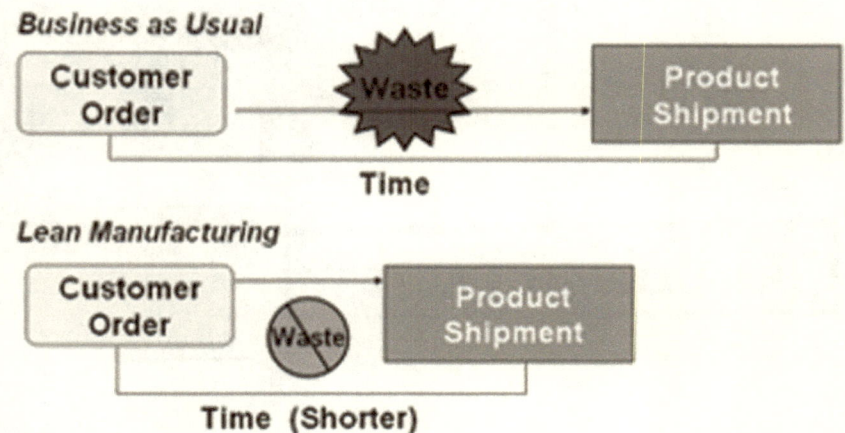

What are the tenets of Lean Manufacturing?

Lean Manufacturing is centered on several basic concepts. As mentioned previously, not every one of them is appropriate or applicable to all organizations. The key is to study the concepts and see which ones are a fit for your organization.

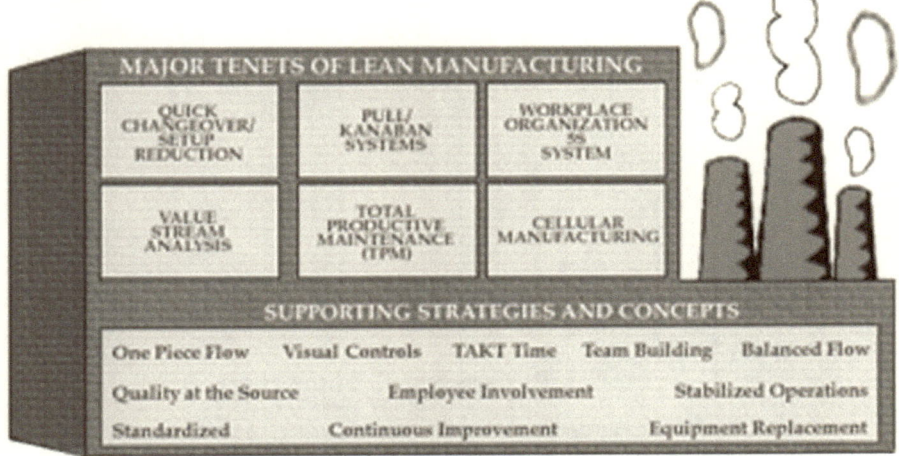

MAJOR TENETS OF LEAN MANUFACTURING

QUICK CHANGEOVER/ SETUP REDUCTION	PULL/ KANABAN SYSTEMS	WORKPLACE ORGANIZATION 5S SYSTEM
VALUE STREAM ANALYSIS	TOTAL PRODUCTIVE MAINTENANCE (TPM)	CELLULAR MANUFACTURING

SUPPORTING STRATEGIES AND CONCEPTS

One Piece Flow	Visual Controls	TAKT Time	Team Building	Balanced Flow
Quality at the Source		Employee Involvement		Stabilized Operations
Standardized		Continuous Improvement		Equipment Replacement

Figure 45 Major Tenets of Lean Manufacturing

1. Quick Changeover/Setup Reduction

In a manufacturing operation with molds and presses that require die changes, a great deal of time is lost every time the die is changed. Often hours are lost during a die changeover. So in order to keep downtime to a minimum, plants build and hold inventory. With SMED, the idea is to do as much of the setup as possible before the line is shut down. In other words, we want to convert internal setup to external setup. The goal of SMED is reduce change overs to "single minute" i.e. 9 minutes or less!

Figure 46, SMED Implementation, illustrates the basic plan beginning with internal and external setup procedures not distinguished. Using these techniques Toyota was able to reduce the changeover on a 1000 ton press from 4 hours to three minutes!

After you have pushed as much of the internal setup as possible to external setup, focus on locking and alignment. Much time is spent making sure dies and jigs are properly aligned and secured. Implement foolproof alignment devices and fast locking procedures. For example, where bolts and nuts must be used, keep in mind the nut only tightens on the last thread! At the very least, use the proper length bolt! Also, in many cases quick release cams may be used! (See Figure 47)

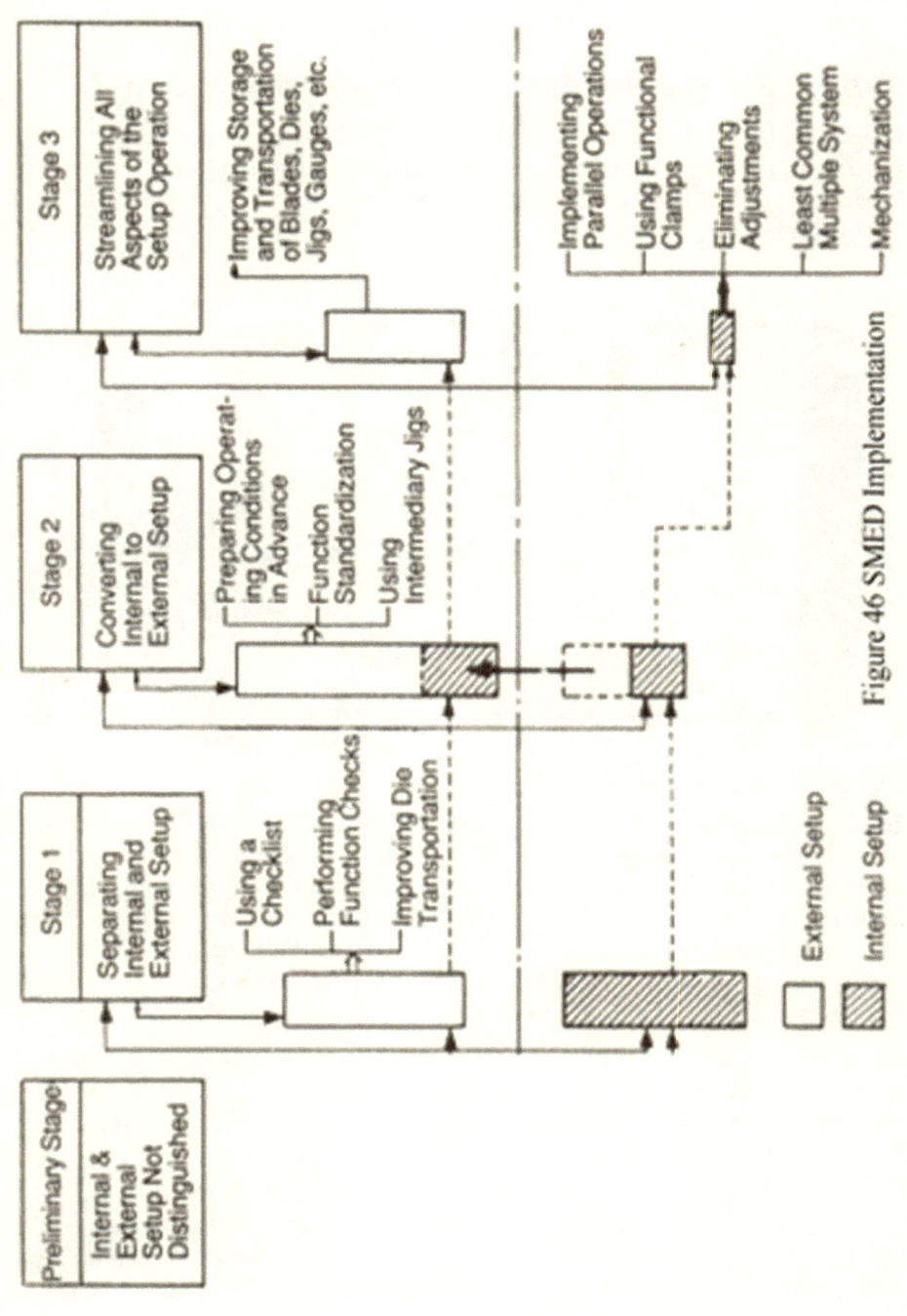

Figure 46 SMED Implementation

Preliminary Stage
Internal & External Setup Not Distinguished

Stage 1 — Separating Internal and External Setup
- Using a Checklist
- Performing Function Checks
- Improving Die Transportation

Stage 2 — Converting Internal to External Setup
- Preparing Operating Conditions in Advance
- Function Standardization
- Using Intermediary Jigs

Stage 3 — Streamlining All Aspects of the Setup Operation
- Improving Storage and Transportation of Blades, Dies, Jigs, Gauges, etc.
- Implementing Parallel Operations
- Using Functional Clamps
- Eliminating Adjustments
- Least Common Multiple System
- Mechanization

External Setup

Internal Setup

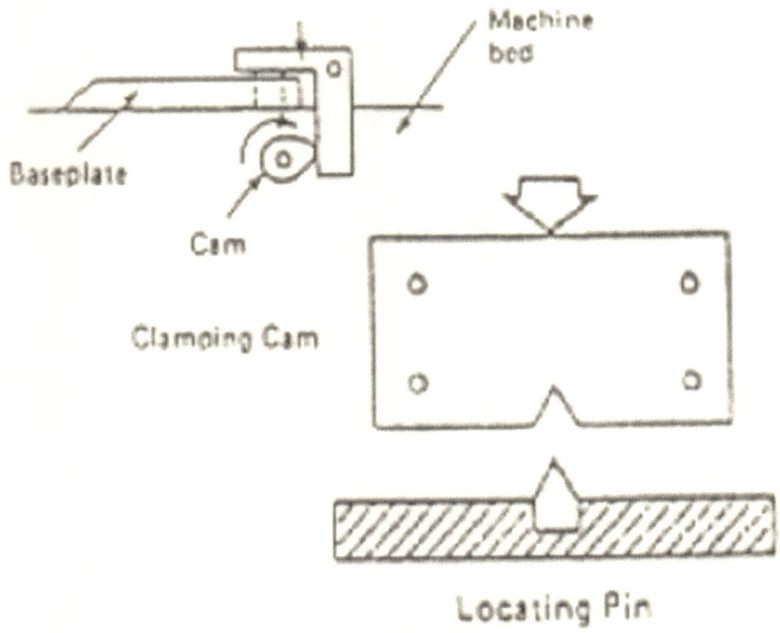

Figure 47 Alignment and locking

2. Kanban System

In most American manufacturing plants, parts are pushed through the system based loosely on customer demand for the final product. What tends to happen is we build up excessive inventory. We convince ourselves that it's better to produce a little extra than to run out of parts when we need them. After all, warehouse space is the cheapest of all... right? So what if all the processes make a little extra and we hold a lot of Work In Progress?

In 1956 Taiichi Ohno visited the United States. He came here to look at our automobile manufacturing plants but was every impressed by our supermarkets. He saw that customers could get exactly what they wanted in the quantity they needed. The supermarket supplied the products in a clean and simple format.

The supermarket concept is fundamental to Lean Manufacturing. The idea is to provide exactly what is needed when it's needed; while not holding excessive inventory. Remember, excessive inventory simply masks the problems in our manufacturing systems. As we reduce the amount of inventory we hold, we expose these problems and can eliminate them one by one. Think of inventory as a lake. Here in East Tennessee, the Tennessee Valley Authority (TVA) is responsible for flood control. Every year they lower the level of the lakes and that exposes the rocks that are just below the surface. The lower the lake level, the more rocks are exposed. (See Figure 48)

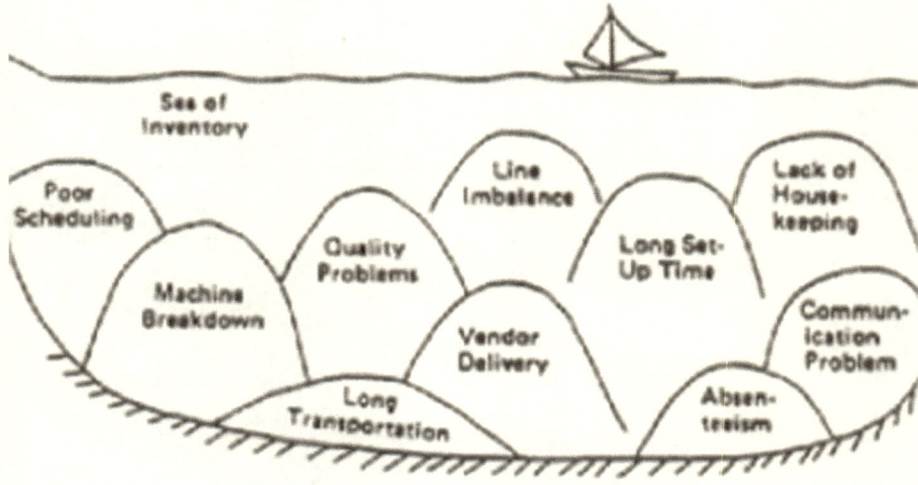

Figure 48 Inventory Covers Problems

With a Kanban system (Signboard) there is literally a plan for every part. We know exactly when the part will be needed, in what quantities, and how we will deliver it to the work cell. The goal is to achieve a balanced, just-in-time production system. One of the critical features of Lean Manufacturing/TPS is the way it links production to real demand. This means it's a pull system rather than the push system we typically see in American manufacturing plants.

The Kanban (usually in the form of cards) has on it such things as: where the parts will be used, quantities, where the parts were produced. Every box of parts has its own Kanban. There are two types of Kanban cards: move and production. See Figure 49 for examples of each.

Nothing moves in the plant without a Kanban. As mention above usually it's a card attached to the box of parts; however, sometimes, it's actually a cart of material. The Kanban is a critical element of the TPS in that is allows each employee to manage their own jobs. The Kanban signals the need for more parts to be delivered to a work cell, thus the individual employee has now become responsible for ordering their own parts.

Types of Information on a Production Kanban Card

 (Appearance)	Part No.	17634-22631-12		Process
	Name of Product	Piston Ring		Machining
	Container Type	S 10C	No. Issued	MC-12
	Container Capacity	200	2/5	

Note: By designating colors for different lines, the handling of Kanban will be easier with fewer materials.

Types of Information on a Move Kanban Card

Process (From)	Storage Location	C-2-3		Process (To)
Factory A	Part No.	17634-22631-12		Factory B
	Name of Part	Piston Ring		
Shipping Post No.	Container Type	S10	No. Issued	Receiving Post No.
Press 107	Container Capacity	200	3/5	Assembly 16

(orange)   Example:
Red = Assembly Line
Blue = Paint
Black = Moulding
Orange = Press

(red)

Figure 49 Kanban Cards

3. Workplace Organization/5S

How important is attitude to the workplace? I read a story once about an American company that had a 107% defect rate! You may wonder, how does a company have a 107% defect rate? The answer is really simple, everything they produced failed inspections and had to be sent to rework and then 7% of what came out of rework still failed inspections!

Needless to say, this company was broke and bankrupt and was going out of business. At the last minute it was bought out by a Japanese company. Within a few months, the defect rate dropped to near zero. What miracle technique did the new Japanese owners bring? Simple – *good housekeeping!* The working conditions were poor; the plant was dirty and even somewhat unsafe. You see the employees had naturally developed a bad attitude. The new owners came in and cleaned the place up – top to bottom and then organized the plant. As the changes took place – and the people were involved in making these changes, their attitudes began to improve. As the employees' attitudes got better the quality of the product improved as well! More than good housekeeping; 5S is a path toward a safer, more efficient, and high performance workplace.

In essence, here is the English translation of what the 5S program is all about:

➤ *Sort* – The people that own the work cell (or area) get together and get rid of all the clutter. If you are not using it, on a routine basis you don't need it in the area. Move it to what is called the "Red Tag Area". Here others can see what is being eliminated and if they need it, they can get it. You also have to use a little common sense. One company near here got rid of a $35,000 machine because they had not needed is in several months. About eight months after they scrapped it, sure enough, they needed it and ended up having to buy another one! The moral is, getting it out of your area is one thing, but you can put things is storage if there is a need for them in the future!

➤ *Set in Order* – Like my Mother used to say, "A place for everything and everything in its place". The team identifies where everything goes and marks it accordingly. Using shadow boards for tools is a typical example of Set in Order.

➤ *Shine* – Here is where the housekeeping really comes in to play. More than just sweeping moping, the operators keep the equipment clean and free from oil and dust. Employees should be given cleanup time at the end of the shift to make sure their area is clean and ready for the next person. They should also be taught that if for some reason, there is some slack time in the schedule, they should garb a broom and dust and be cleaning – not just standing around!

> *Standardize* – This means we will standardize our procedures, making sure we are all on the same page, so to speak.

> *Sustain* – Keep it up! That is one of the most difficult things to do at first. It's very easy to start something; but the real question is can you – will you – keep it up when things start to get a little rough. All too often when the going gets tough, we fall back on our old ways of doing things.

4. *Value Stream Mapping (Process Analysis)*

The concept of Process Mapping or Value Stream Mapping has its roots with the work of Fredrick Taylor and his search for "one best way" to perform a job. Taylor thought it was management's job to find that best way. Frank Gilbreth was one of Taylor's associates and developed the first process mapping system know as "Process Charting". He viewed all work as a process and he developed many of the symbols that are still in use today. And as a footnote, the original movie version of "Cheaper by the Dozen" was based on his life.

Gilbreth

Value Stream Mapping is a process-mapping method that enables your organization to:

- Working from the customer backwards, examine the flow of information and work in process needed to produce a product or service

- Understand where the largest sources of waste (non-value added activity) are in the value stream and envision a less wasteful future state

- Develop implementation plans for future Lean activities

In the book Lean Thinking, James P. Womack and Daniel T. Jones defined value stream mapping as: "Identification of all the specific activities occurring in a value stream for a product or product family" Value stream mapping is a tool for understanding how information and materials flow between processes to deliver value to a customer. Taking a "big-picture," customer-oriented view of an organization's activities allows Lean implementers to identify and prioritize future improvement efforts. The Value Stream Mapping information is

courtesy of Strategos, Inc., for more information please visit
www.strategosinc.com.

Typical steps in value stream mapping include:

1. Select a product family
2. Collect data on the current state of the value stream
3. Draw a current state value stream map, identifying waste (non-value-added activity) in the value stream
4. Brainstorm ideas to improve production flow, meet customer demand (Takt time – the heartbeat of the process), and level product mix
5. Draw a future state value stream map, highlighting targets for Lean improvement efforts
6. Develop a kaizen implementation plan

The Current State Map

The Current State Map is, as the name implies, a visual representation of the process as it is now. Working from the customer backwards (internal customer or external customer – for the big picture), a careful analysis must be conducted and every step, each arm movement, all delays must be clearly documented.

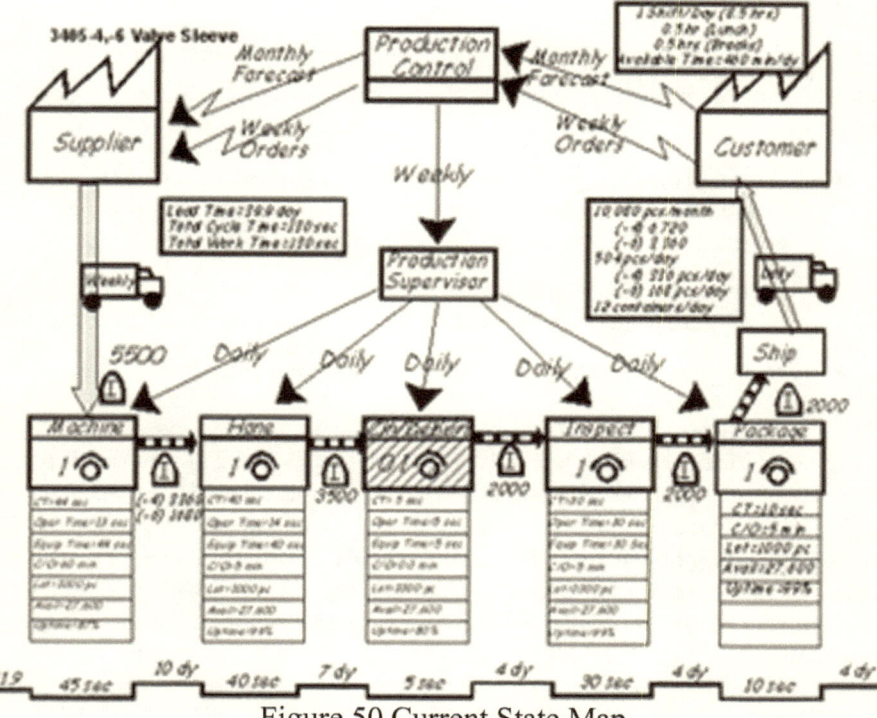

Figure 50 Current State Map

While the completed map looks complex, intimidating, and confusing, it's really very simple when drawn step-by-step.

Step 1: Draw in Customer, Supplier, and Production Control

Step 2: Enter customer requirements by month and by day. If customer orders are infrequent batches, then note batch size and frequency

Step: 3 Calculate daily production and container requirements. When containers hold multiple pieces, calculate number of containers.

Figure 51 Present State Map Steps 1, 2, and 3

Step 4: Draw outbound shipping icon & delivery frequency; note full, partial, or mixed loads.

Step 5: Draw outbound shipping icon & delivery frequency; note full, partial, or mixed loads.

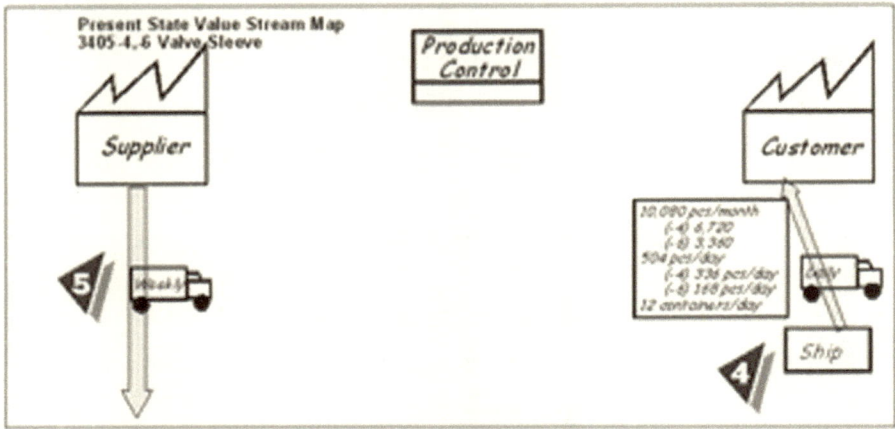

Figure 52 Present State Map Steps 4 and 5

Step 6: Draw boxes for each process from left to right.

Step 7: Add data boxes below the process boxes and the time line for value added and now value added.

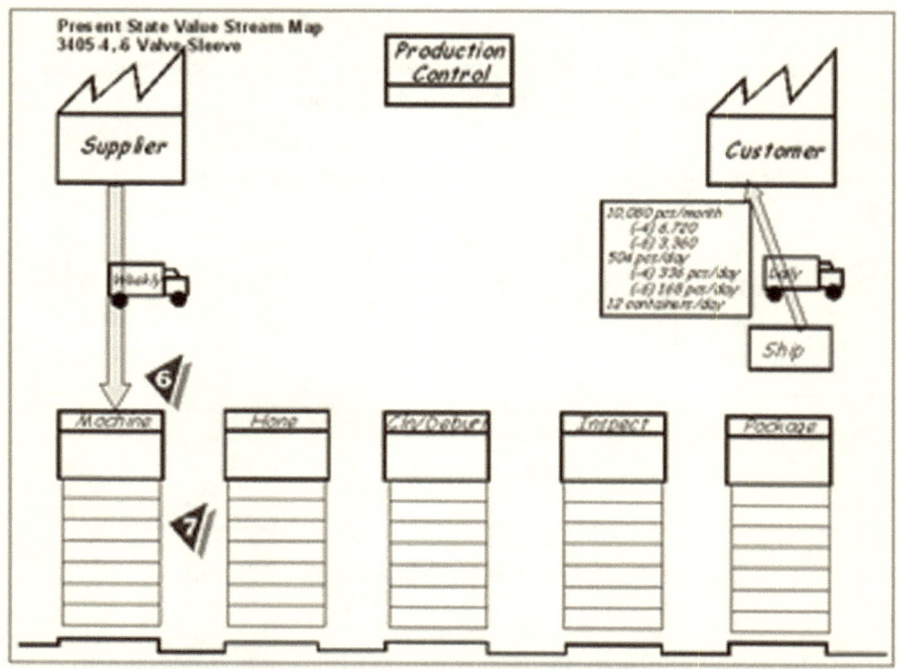

Figure 53 Present State Map Steps 6 and 7

Figure 54 illustrates the key symbols that you will find on a Current State Map. The Appendix contains many more common symbols. The Data Box under each Process Box provides important information and can include the following information:

Number of people required for the operation

Cycle Time (C/T) – Time required to produce a single unit

Operator Time (O/T) – Time operator is occupied to produce a single item

Equipment Time (E/T) – Time equipment is occupied to produce a single item

Change Over Time (C/O) – Time from the last piece of one product to the fist good piece of a subsequent product.

Lot Size – How may pieces required for a production run

Available – Total time per day the work station is available

Scrap – The amount of scrap produced

Uptime – The average percentage of time the workstation operates

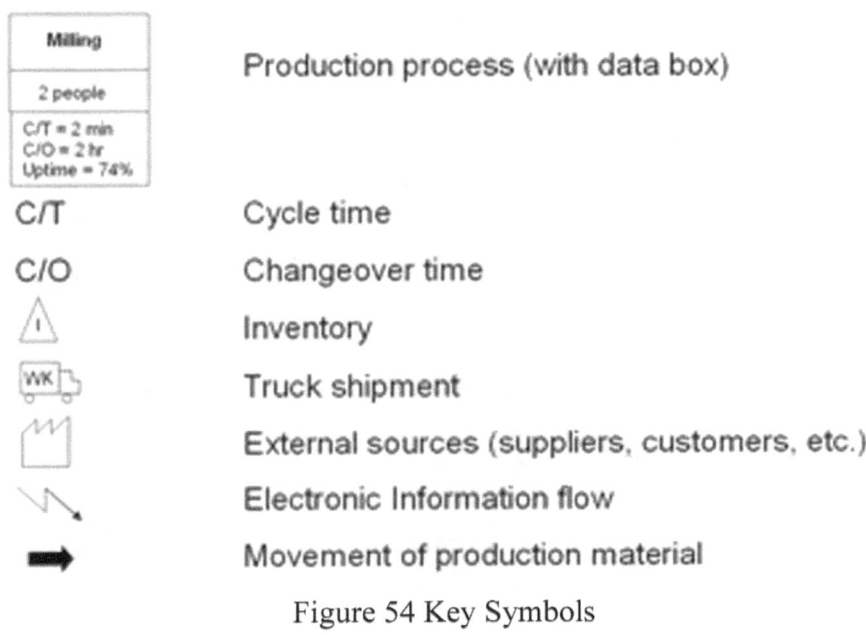

Production process (with data box)

C/T   Cycle time

C/O   Changeover time

Inventory

Truck shipment

External sources (suppliers, customers, etc.)

Electronic Information flow

Movement of production material

Figure 54 Key Symbols

Figure 55 illustrates a completely fill out Process and Data Box. In this example, the process is Hone and it requires one operator. The cycle time is 40 seconds. It takes the operator 14 seconds to finish one product. The equipment operates for 40 seconds to produce one product. When change overs are required, it takes 5 minutes from the end one production run to the first good piece of the new run. Lot size is 1000 pieces. The machine is available for 27,600 seconds a day with an average up time of 99%.

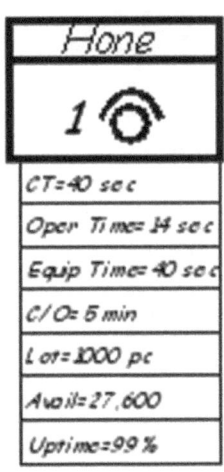

Figure 55
Data Box

Step 8: Add communication arrows note methods and frequency.

Step 9: Add the process attributes to the Data Boxes.

Step 10: Add Operator Symbol (may be indicated by a fraction of an operator if several processes are run by one operator at the same time.

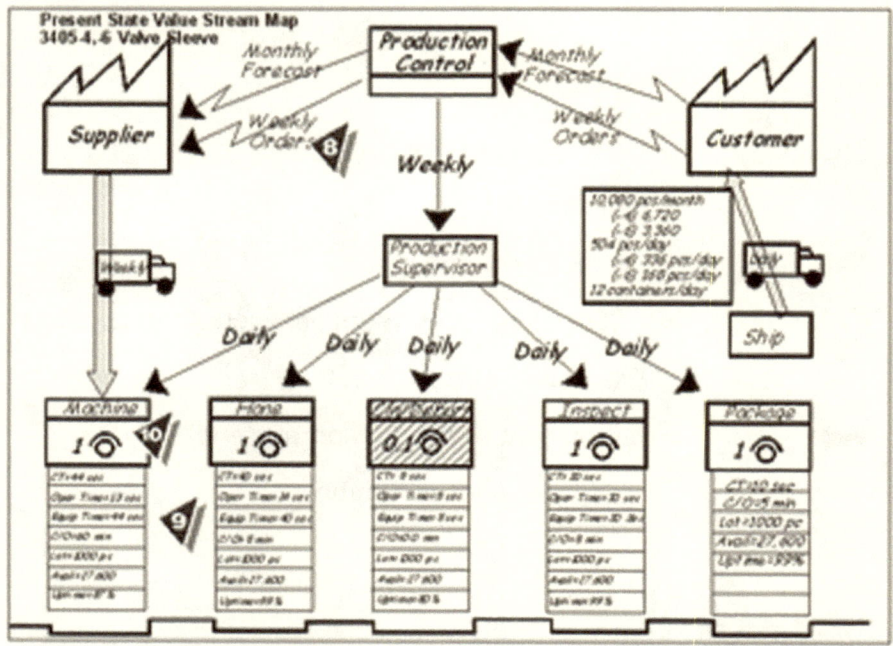

Figure 56 Present State Map Steps 8, 9, and 10

Step 11: Add inventory locations and levels (in units). In order to calculate the amount of inventory at each work station, we need to estimate the average inventory. You should go out and actually count the inventory and not depend on estimates or the amount that "should be there." Next divide the average inventory by the daily production rate for that item. This gives you the number of days of inventory on hand. This calculation is based on Little's Law, and is illustrated in Figure 57.

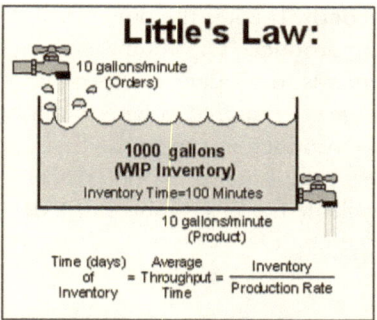

Figure 57 Lead Time

Step 12: Add push, pull, and FIFO icons. These show how inventory is handled between process boxes. Figure 58 illustrates the typical inventory systems.

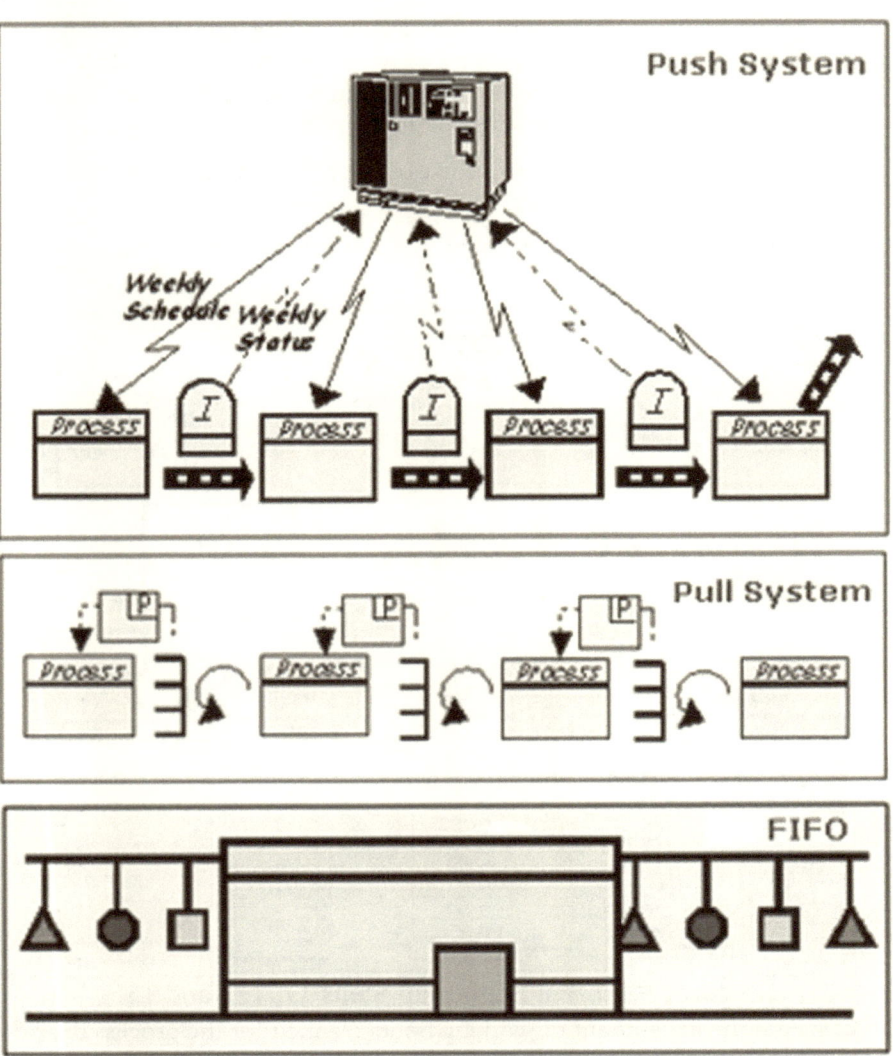

Figure 58 Inventory Management Systems

> Push – A push system is the conventional type of inventory management system such as MRP. A schedule goes out to all the processes and all start working at the same time. When a particular process experiences a problem, other area of the plant are not aware the problem exists and continue to work according to the original

schedule. Individual process fluctuations demand large inventories be maintained in order meet scheduling demands.

➢ Pull – The pull system places a small amount of inventory for each process in a central location called a Kanban stock point or supermarket. A downstream process takes what it needs and an upstream process replaces it. This system works very well in situations where a process must produce multiple parts in small batches.

➢ FIFO – FIFO simply means First In First Out. An example of this would be parts moving on a conveyor system.

Step 13: Add any additional information that you believe you will find useful to the analysis.

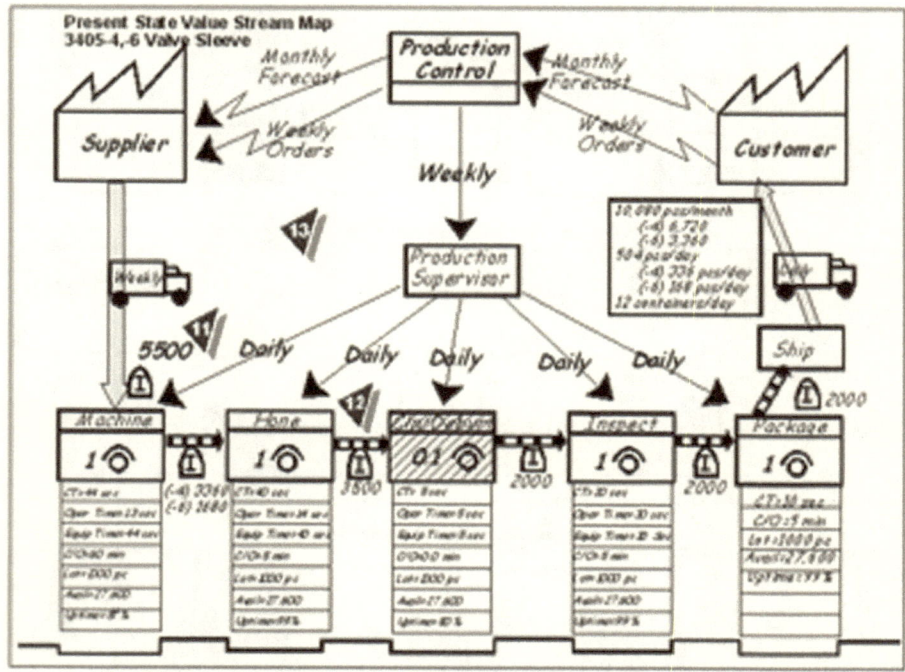

Figure 59 Present State Map Steps 11, 12, and 13

Step 14: Add the net amount of working hours planned for the process or department, based on expected customer demand.

Step 15: Determine the lead times. These times are determined from the information contained in the process Data blocks and includes: setup, person, machine, and cycle (or process) times.

Step 16: Determine the total cycle time and lead time and then place them on the time line at the bottom of the process map.

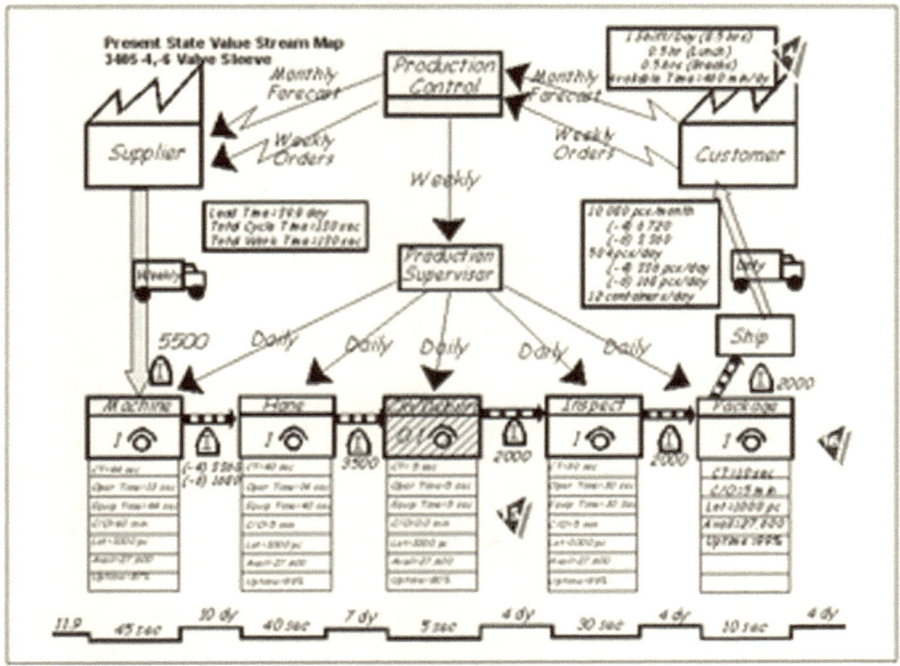

Figure 60 Present State Map Steps 14, 15, and 16

Future State Map

After a complete understanding of the current process, you ready to begin the ongoing Kaizen strategy of process improvement. The Future State map (See Figure 62) is the vision of where you want the process to be. Visualize the types of improvements that can take place. Creating the Future State Map, and moving your organization in that direction requires a thorough understanding of the concepts of Lean Manufacturing. Keep in mind, the goal is not to create a perfect, detailed, roadmap to the future. The goal is it to explore the possibilities. This is a work in progress and there will be changes made as new ideas are implemented and we learn more about the process.

Step 1: Review the Current State Map. Make sure that the flow is correct and everyone agrees and understands the process. It is not necessary that team members agree on every minor detail. Then ask the team to look for areas where there may be improvements. Look for long lead times and high inventory. Are there quality problems?

Step 2: Calculate Takt Time. Takt Time is like the heartbeat of the process. It is based on customer demand. Takt Time is the pace of production needed to meet customer demand. Compare the Takt time to the Process Time for each process. The goal is to produce to demand. In any process where Process Time exceeds Takt Time, there is currently a capacity problem.

Net Operating Time Per Sift:	Shift: 8 hours X 60 minutes = 480 min	480	
	Breaks: 2 @ 15 minutes =	-30	
	Cleanup: 1 @ 5 minutes =	-5	
	Net operating time per shift =	445	Minutes
	445 Minutes x 60 seconds/minute =	26,700	Seconds

Customer Requirements: # Units/day =   530 Units

$$\text{Takt Time} = \frac{\text{Your Operating Time per Shift}}{\text{Customer Requirement per Shift}}$$

For 1 Shift/day: Takt Time = 26,700 / 530 =   50.4 seconds per unit

Step 3: Identify bottleneck processes. A bottleneck process is one that has the longest cycle time. The bottleneck process determines total system throughput. {In the past, when techniques such as the Critical Path Method (CPM) were used, this would have been called the critical path – the longest path through the process and it determined the time necessary to complete the project.}

Step 4: Identify Lot Size and Setup Opportunities. Small lot sizes (i.e. batches) are critical to the implementation of Lean Manufacturing practices. In fact, in an ideal environment, the lot size would be equal to one unit and the employee simply hands the finished part to the next person on the line!

However, as people that live and work in the real world know, this is far from a perfect world. Little real direction is given in determining lot size in Lean Manufacturing practices, so I suggest we take a look at a technique that was developed almost 100 years ago to calculate how much inventory a company should maintain. This technique is called Economic Order Quantity (EOQ) and it can be adapted to fit today's Lean Manufacturing needs. (The EOQ model was originally developed by F. W. Harris in 1913, though R. H. Wilson is credited for his early in-depth analysis of the model.)

EOQ is a technique to allow you to balance inventory carrying costs and setup costs in order to determine at an optimum lot size. Calculating EOQ can certainly be beneficial in situations where setup and changeover costs remain high and larger batch sizes are required. (See Figure 61)

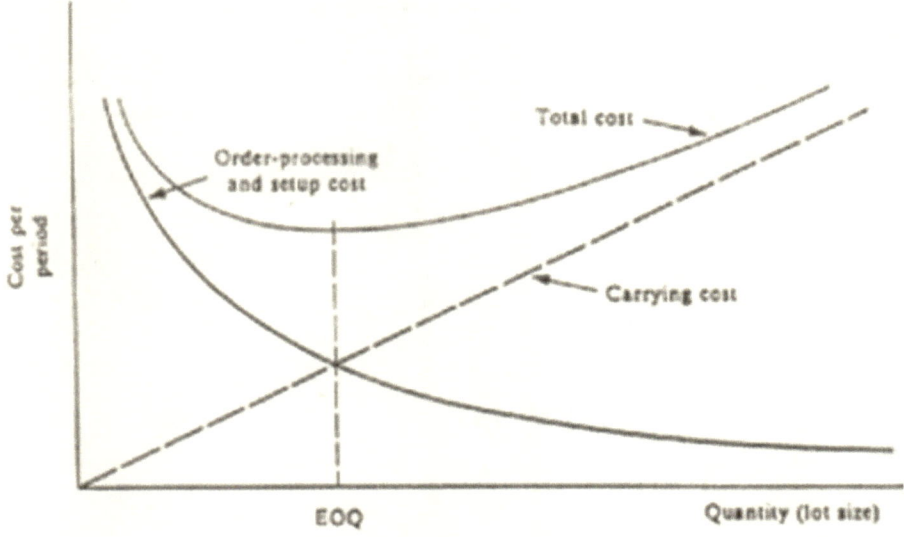

Figure 61 Economic Order Quantity

Since we are looking at two cost curves and our goal is to balance carrying costs with order processing and setup costs, we can add the two curves together and generate a total cost curve. In order to minimize overall costs, we would attempt to order parts (lot sizes) at the minimum point on the total cost curve.

EOQ Variables:

- Q = optimal order quantity

- C = cost per order event (not per unit)

- R = monthly (annual) demand of the product

- P = purchase cost per unit

- F = carrying cost factor; the factor of the purchase cost that is used as the carrying cost (this is usually set at 10-15%, though circumstances can require any setting from 0 to 1)

- H = carrying cost per unit per month (per year) (H = PF)

Carefully consider the variables such as Ordering Costs. Often references may be made to these costs being $100 or more per ordering event. While this may be the case if outside overseas venders are used, your situation may be entirely different. You may be using a local vender, or you may be ordering the parts from an internal supplier if that is the case your costs may be substantially lower; perhaps in the range of $20 to $30. The moral is, don't just plug in some numbers from an industry trade magazine. Spend some time and get accurate information for your unique situation.

$$EOQ = \sqrt{\frac{2(\text{Annual usage in units})(\text{Order cost})}{(\text{Annual carrying cost per unit})}}$$

$$Q^* = \sqrt{\frac{2CR}{PF}} = \sqrt{\frac{2CR}{H}}$$

The superscript asterisk (*) indicates the optimal order quantity.

Step 5: Identify Potential Work Cells. Generally speaking, it's best to group all of the processes of a product into a single work cell. However, for cost and technology reasons this is not always feasible. For example, the operation of some expensive, large scale equipment is not easily scaled down. Additionally, multiple products may have to be processed by this equipment. So for size, cost, or even safety reasons, it is not always possible to locate equipment in a desired work cell.

Step 6: Determine Kanban and FIFO locations. Recall that FIFO processes all of the orders in the same sequence; it's like a traditional assembly line. The Kanban strategy allows for differences in both sequence and batch size!

Step 7: Establish Overall Scheduling Methods. For the most part, the more frequent the scheduling, the better and faster information is generated and transferred, the more efficient production becomes, and the less inventory is required.

Step 8: Calculate New Lead and Cycle Times. To obtain total lead time, add all the values on the time line. To calculate total cycle time add the totals from all the process boxes.

Step 9: Add Kaizen Bursts. As we developed the Future State Map, we made assumptions concerning necessary improvements and omitted the details of these improvements. *Use the Kaizen Burst to illustrate where future work is necessary to implement theses improvements.*

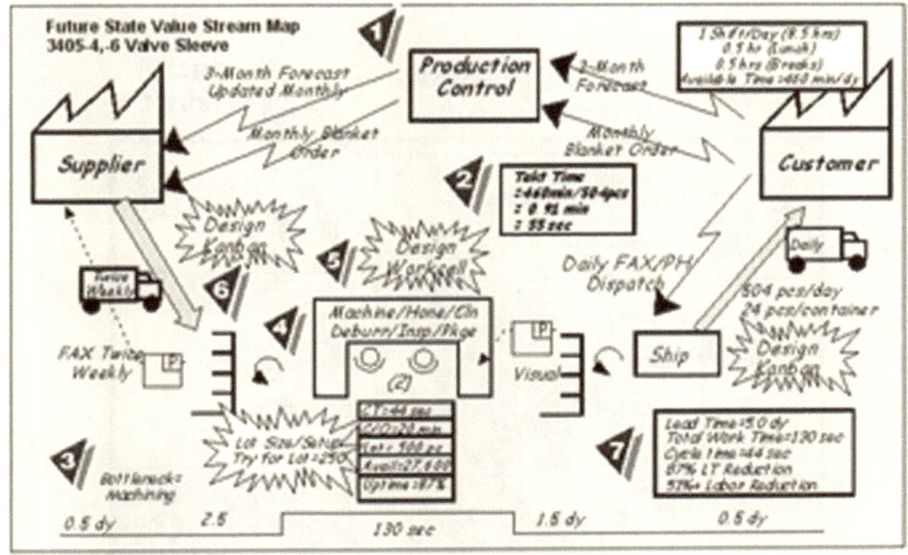

Figure 62 Future State Map

5. Total Productive Maintenance (TPM)

TPM is related to and came from the original concepts of W. Edwards Deming and the Total Quality Management (TQM) philosophy. TPM combines predictive and preventative maintenance with problem solving and total quality. When the concept of Preventative Maintenance was first introduced to Japan, the basic idea was to emphasize the importance of maintenance and bring it in line with TQM concepts. Nippondenso was among the first Japanese to begin implementing a TPM program in the 1960's.

With TPM, maintenance is brought to center stage. No longer are maintenance activities simply squeezed in at the last minute when there is a break in the production schedule. Maintenance "downtime" is planned for as a part of the daily production. The fundamental goal is to be able to hold emergency repairs and other unscheduled maintenance to an absolute minimum.

According to Jack Roberts, TPM is a maintenance program and includes several key aspects: (1) total commitment to the program by upper level management is required, (2) employees must be empowered to initiate corrective action, and (3) a long range outlook must be accepted as TPM may take a year or more to implement and is an on-going process. Changes in employee mind-set toward their job responsibilities must take place as well.

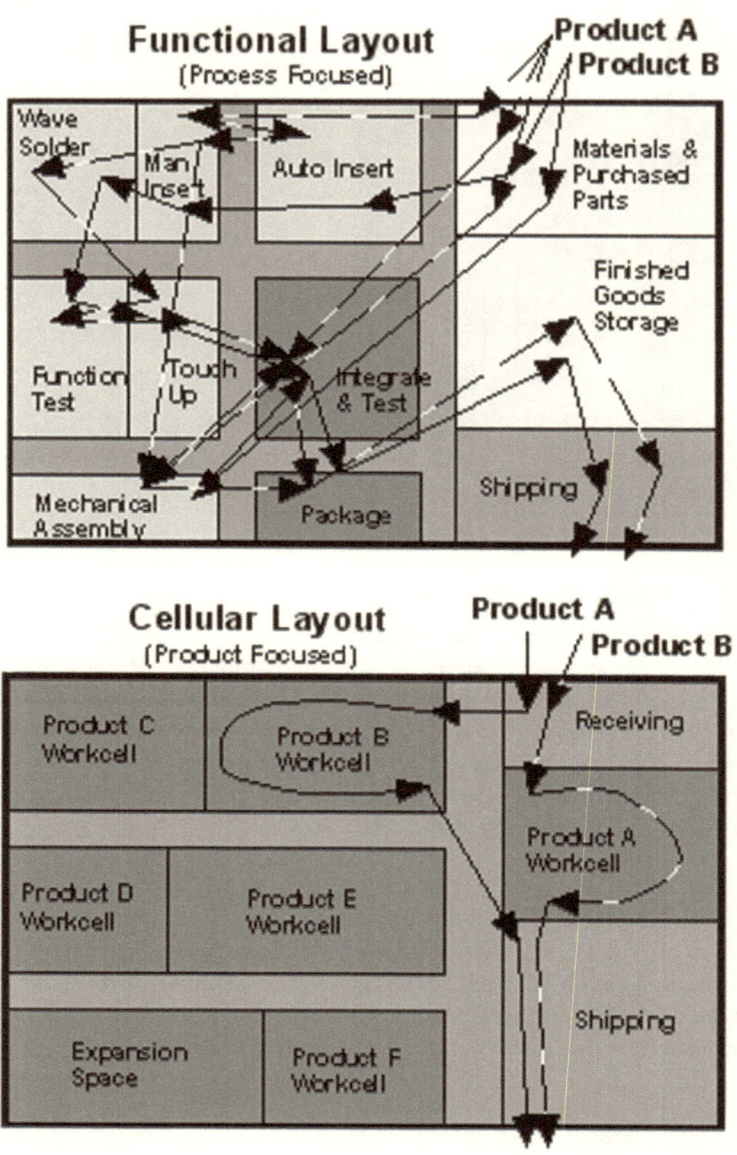

Figure 63 Functional Vs. Cellular Layout

6. Cellular Manufacturing

The purpose of the Cell Manufacturing concept (Figure 63 Functional vs. Cellular Layout) is to simplify workflow and focus our attention on a single product or a very narrow product family. At a minimum quality and inventory are heavily influenced. It organizes work into small groups of 3 to 12 people and 5 to 15 workstations. In a perfect world, the product is completed before leaving the cell. The work cell is at the very heart of Lean Manufacturing. The underlying theme is simplicity.

Typical manufacturing plants are designed along functional lines. Products are moved from one functional area to another in large batches. Bottlenecks occur and inventory backs up. With the cell concept, all work on a product is done in the cell for that product. Batch sizes are smaller and if a bottle neck occurs, the problem is readily identified and corrected.

A Final Note About Lean Manufacturing

It is far beyond the scope of this book to delve into more specifics of workstation design, visual management indicators, line stop, and Cellular Manufacturing. The main goal has been to provide the reader with a solid background into the concepts of Lean Manufacturing, not to make them an overnight expert. Entire books have been written on this subject and certainly we can not hope to accomplish in one chapter what others have expounded upon for hundreds of pages.

"What this power is I cannot say; all I know is that it exists and it becomes available only when a man is in that state of mind in which he knows exactly what he wants and is fully determined not to quit until he finds it."

Alexander Graham Bell

Chapter 12:
Building a Success
Mindset

You can learn all you can about Total Quality Leadership, Deming, Lean Culture/Manufacturing, and SPC. You can become the Total Quality Champion at your organization. You can hire the best consultants to train the employees and re-design processes. However, unless you are able to build teams of empowered associates, the cultural changes necessary to achieve true success will not be realized. It is *absolutely fundamental* to have the front line employees involved in this effort from the very beginning. If they are not a part of the program, they will feel like this is just something else that management is trying to ram down their throats.

We've talked a little about getting your people involved in the improvement process by using team meetings and brain storming techniques. Going beyond that, how do you *inspire and motivate* people to join together to make this effort a success? This chapter is devoted to motivation and success. For the most part, everything up to now has been philosophy, strategy, tools, and techniques; now we are going to look at the very heart and soul of the engine that drives the success of a company – motivated teams!

Traditional Motivation

For me, Maslow's Hierarchy of Needs is still fundamental to understanding and motivating people. In essence, Maslow said that people are motivated by many unsatisfied needs. We do things in life to obtain satisfaction of those needs. Those needs fall into several categories including:

- ➢ Basic – Food, clothing, shelter
- ➢ Security – Having a job, providing for the future
- ➢ Social – Having friends, being accepted

- ➢ Self-Esteem – The desire for status and position
- ➢ Self-Actualization – The desire to be all you are capable of becoming

Maslow said we act on the needs in a stair step fashion and as soon as one need is at least partially satisfied, we move on to the next one. *A satisfied need is no longer a motivator!* (Maslow, 1943)

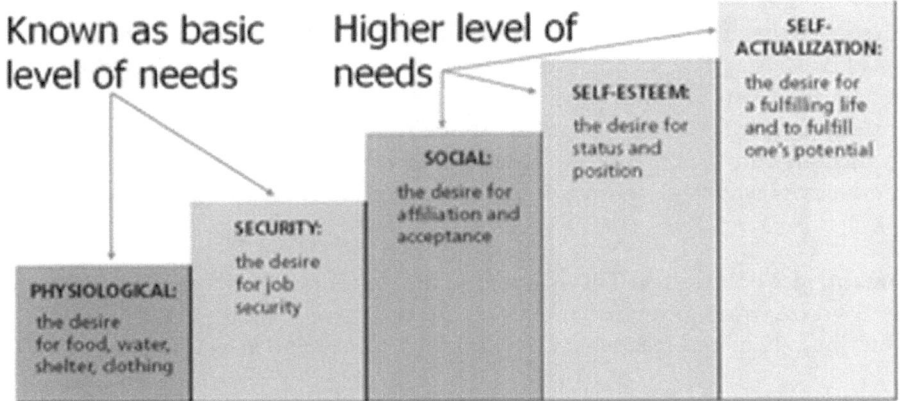

Supervisors tend to think employees are at the basic need level, when in reality they are often operating at the higher need levels.

Figure 64 Maslow's Hierarchy of Needs

Generally speaking, the first two levels of needs are satisfied by having a job. Almost any fulltime job in America will at least partially satisfy the first two basic needs. When that happens, the basic needs are no longer primary motivators. *Make no mistake, money is important at every need level and you must offer a decent, market competitive, wage in order to attract and retain better educated employees.*

Most supervisors make the false assumption that people are at the basic needs level and are only motivated by money. Because they believe money is the primary motivator and there is little they can do to get the employee more money, they typically do little to attempt to motivate their team. However, this is not the case, most people are operating from the higher need levels and it's up to the supervisors to figure out what each employee's needs are and help them satisfy those needs. For example, what can a supervisor do to satisfy an employee's need for self-esteem? Or what if an employee is operating at the highest need level, the need for self-actualization – the need to be all they are capable of becoming?

Fear Techniques: Even today many supervisors still try to motivate employees using fear techniques. They believe that they can make people obey the rules and do their jobs by using threats. They will typically tell people things like, "This is not a popularity contest, I am here to make sure you do you job!" They also usually close by saying, "And if you don't like it here – you know where the door is!"

They use this technique because it's simple, easy to use, makes them feel good (they love the power), but most importantly, *they use fear techniques because they work!* Yes, using fear techniques do work, for short periods of time and in certain situations. People have a "thick skin" they will put up with the yelling and the threats for awhile; however, after a time, people will get fed up and quit! In the long run, using fear techniques will lower morale, increase turnover, productivity will drop, and the defect and scrap rates will go up dramatically.

Incentive Techniques: This is a step in the right direction. I mean, at least now we are trying to reward employees for doing something right, instead of punishing them and creating an environment of fear and insecurity.

However, incentive motivation techniques are not without their shortcomings. For example, incentive techniques usually give promise to all, but in reality there's going to be a limited number of winners. In fact, the top performers are usually the winners – so the top 10% of the team gets excited about the new reward program, while the remaining 90% become de-motivated at the thought of, "Here we go again, another game and it's going to be either Jim or Carol that gets the prize; they always win." What a great motivational program, I just motivated the top people and de-motivated the rest of my team.

Often, progressively higher and higher rewards have to be offered just to maintain the same level of performance. Incentives are usually external and short lived. The motivation lasts about as long as it takes to spend the bonus – or until the "new" wears off. That's one of the reasons why in the last 100 years, benefits have grown from less that 5% of a wage package to more than 50% of a wage package. *With incentives and bonuses, people always want more!*

Finally, what starts out as a reward for good performance, in good times, often becomes a right in the mind of the employee. For example, let's say that a company gives a $500 bonus at Christmas. Well, they do this for a number of years; however, one year, costs are up, productivity is down, and the general economy is sluggish, so they decide to eliminate the bonus. Can you imagine the revolt they would have on their hands? In fact, years ago, I read about a company that had been giving their employees turkeys at Thanksgiving. They had done this for a number of years. One year they decided not to. The employees got so mad they sued the company! They flied a class action lawsuit over turkeys! And if you think that's crazy, then consider this – they won! You see, the turkeys had become an implied part of the employee's compensation package and the company could not just stop giving them out at Thanksgiving.

Self-motivation: External motivation techniques such as fear and incentives are invariability short lived. The only motivation technique that will last is internal, self-motivation. Self-motivation is predicated on change; however, the change comes from inside the person – not from outside! Self-motivation is created through the effective use of goal setting. As a leader, I can't really motivate people; at best, all I can do is remove the organizational barriers and help people motivate themselves.

Who motivates the motivator? That's an age old question. The answer is really simple. Before you can motivate a team you have to be able to motivate *yourself!*

What does success mean to you?

Success is Personal: According to Paul J. Meyer, "Success is the progressive realization of worthwhile, predetermined, personal goals." That has to be one of the best definitions of success I have ever seen. Most definitions say something along the lines of "one that succeeds" or "the successful termination of a venture". The problem is you can't define a word, by using that word in the definition. Let's think about what this really means.

Progressive Realization: Success is the result of a lifelong process of goal setting. When I was growing up, my parents told me to set goals, teachers told me to set goals, the Air Force told me to set goals – but *no one ever told me how to set goals* and there definitely is a right way to set goals! New Years Resolutions generally don't work! Why should we wait for one day of the year to set a goal? When I was conducting public training programs, I used to ask people how long their New Year Resolutions lasted. I got a wide range of responses. Some people said days, even weeks. And some people did stick to the resolution until they achieved the goal. I have to admit, my favorite response – one I got on several occasions was, "How long did my New Years Resolution last; till I sobered up!"

Worthwhile: Have you ever had something you wanted to do? The more you thought about it, the more convinced you became. Finally, you told someone you cared about. They listened to you and then no sooner had your mouth stopped moving, they tilted their head to one side and said, "That's got to be the craziest thing I have ever heard! Why do you want to do something like that? You could lose your money – waste your time – get hurt..." So, because you respected them, you listened to them and they killed one of your dreams. And the sad fact is, *when your dreams die a piece of you dies right along with them!* These people had your best interest at heart, they did not want to see you make a mistake; however, it was not important to them, it was not worthy of their efforts. However, it was important to you.

Because my parents always gave me emotional support as I was growing up, when people told me I was crazy for wanting to do something, I never let that bother me – if it was important to me, I did it. They instilled in me the belief that *there is no substitute for excellence and there is no room for failure.* People thought I was crazy when I wanted to design and build a passive solar, earth sheltered home and live "off the grid". (Off the grid meaning I used no commercially generated electricity). This type of lifestyle is not for everyone, but it was the right choice for me and my family. We did not let the naysayers talk us out of our dreams and goals and to that end we built the A-Frame home my Dad wanted and our passive solar, earth sheltered home. From 1984 until 2001 we lived as energy independently as possible! We did hook up to the electric grid in 2001. The low head water turbine we used to produce our electricity needed to be replaced and the simple truth was, because of climate change and diminishing rainfall amounts, the creek did not flow as strong as it used to and I was having to run a backup generator more and more often. So, now I do pay an electric bill. The almost 2000 square foot home is still very energy efficient and my total electric bill is only around $40 a month!

Predetermined: Success is rarely the result of an accident. I am not going to be an overnight success. I am not going to be an overnight millionaire. The odds of me being an overnight millionaire go up dramatically when I actually buy a lottery ticket – but since I rarely ever buy a ticket, the odds remain real low! It took me years to design and build both the hydroelectric system and the earth sheltered home. Proper planning is essential to success. As a SCUBA diving instructor, one of the key rules I taught was to, "Always plan your dive and dive your plan." Without predetermined goals in your life, you are like a ship drifting aimlessly on the sea of life.

Personal Goals: The goals you set for yourself must be personal to you. The goals you set must reflect your personal beliefs, standards, and desires. Unless your goals are personal to you, you will not be able to maintain your interest in them. This is especially true in business. Business goals must be internalized by you or you will not give all you can give to the completion of the goals. At best, you will only work half-heartily.

A Formula for Success

There is a Formula for Success that anyone can apply. It really isn't all that difficult, but it does take commitment and determination. Are you ready to do more than dream of success? Are you ready to inspire and help motivate others to personal and professional success?

Self-awareness – Where are you on the roadmap of life?

There's an old saying, "If you don't know where you are going, any road will get you there!" You must know where you are today, *before* you can get to where you want to go tomorrow. If I was going to plan a trip, I'd look at a map. But, when you first pick up the map, do you find your destination and then look at where you are starting from? Of course not; the first thing you do is look to see *exactly* where you are on the map right now.

Now in the high tech world of today, we may not use a map – we might go to the internet and visit MapQuest©. But still, the first thing MapQuest© asks is what is your starting location; then it asks for your destination. Let's say, for example, I was going to drive to Las Vegas, NV. I've never been, so this might make a great road trip.

I enter my starting point, Morristown, TN and my ending point of Las Vegas and then all I have to do is to push a button and I get turn-by-turn directions that will guide me on my trip!

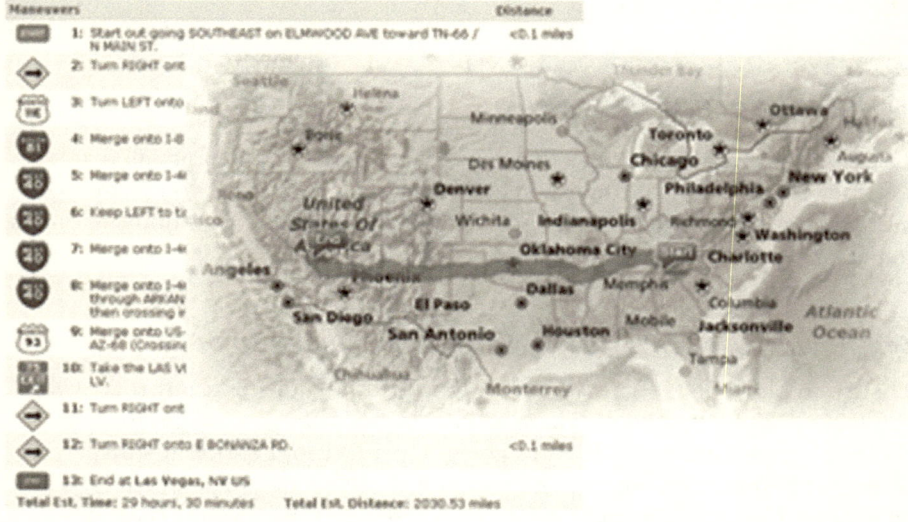

Maneuvers		Distance
	1: Start out going SOUTHEAST on ELMWOOD AVE toward TN-66 / N MAIN ST.	<0.1 miles
	2: Turn RIGHT ont	
	3: Turn LEFT onto	
	4: Merge onto I-8	
	5: Merge onto I-4	
	6: Keep LEFT to ta	
	7: Merge onto I-4	
	8: Merge onto I-4 through ARKAN then crossing i	
	9: Merge onto US-AZ-68 (Crossin	
	10: Take the LAS VI LV.	
	11: Turn RIGHT ont	
	12: Turn RIGHT onto E BONANZA RD.	<0.1 miles
	13: End at Las Vegas, NV US	

Total Est. Time: 29 hours, 30 minutes   Total Est. Distance: 2030.53 miles

So, my route is clearly identified and I can see it will take me 29 hours and 30 minutes and I will travel approximately 2030.53 miles! *Wouldn't it be great if finding our way in life was that simple?* Well, it almost is – and the first step is self-awareness, knowing where we are today.

Allow me to introduce you to the Living Wheel. The Living Wheel is a simple way for us to judge our satisfaction with the six major areas of our life:

- Career
- Health
- Educational
- Home
- Spiritual
- Social

Here's what I want you to do. Get a clean sheet of paper and put a dot in the center of the page. Next draw a large circle around that dot. Finally, draw six spokes on the wheel. Now you've just created an old fashion wagon wheel. Next, I want you to label each spoke with one of the areas of life. (Figure 65)

the Living Wheel

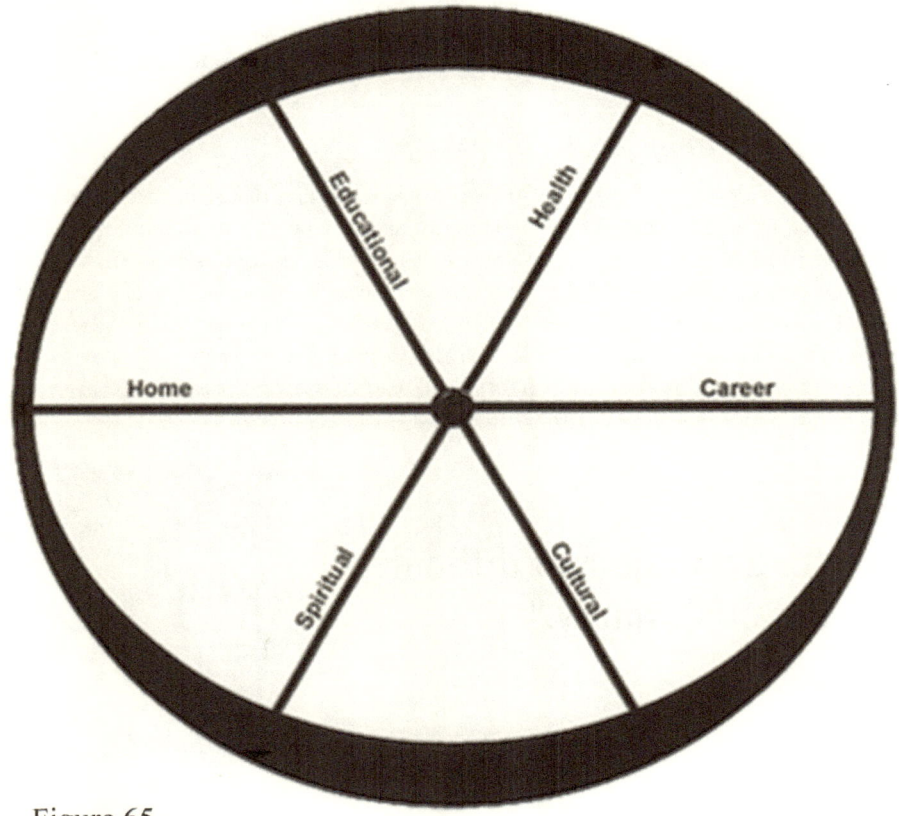

Figure 65

Finally, judge your satisfaction with where you are in each area of life. Put a dot on each spoke representing your satisfaction with that area of your life. If you are not satisfied with an area of life, put the dot on the spoke near the hub. As your satisfaction increases, put the dot on the spoke nearer the rim. If you were 100% satisfied you would place the dot on the rim! Don't take a lot of time and use your first impressions. It's important to be completely honest with yourself.

After you have put a dot on each spoke representing your satisfaction with that area of life, go back and connect the dots. When you have connected all the dots, stop and ask yourself, "How well does my wheel roll?" Don't be surprised if your wheel is lopsided and has flat spots! That's just human nature. People tend to get focused on certain areas that are important to them and then they neglect other areas. The key here is that in just a few minutes you have taken the time to identify some areas of your life you are not happy with. For many of you, this may have been the first time you have stopped and ask yourself how satisfied you are with your life. The next steps are up to you. Are you willing to commit to make the changes to bring you the things you want in life? I will promise you this, if you do set goals and commit to achieving those goals and you do this exercise again in 6 months, your wheel will roll much better!

A Decision to Change

The second step in the Formula for Success is making a decision to change. "You have to want to change." How many times have you heard that? Wanting to change is not enough; you must have a burning desire to make the changes you say are important to you and your life. Remember, it's not enough to make a New Years Resolution – they usually fail. You must learn to be proactive and not just reactive to the world around you. Become a "take charge" person and make things happen instead of sitting there wondering what happened. Look for new opportunities and set goals often!

"In the middle of difficulty lies opportunity."
Albert Einstein

Take Action

Remember, only you can "just do it!" I can help you with self-awareness and I can help you make a decision to change; but only you can take the actions necessary to make the changes you want to make in your life. Like the old saying goes, "You can lead a horse to water, but you can't make them drink". The fountain of success is there in front of you, are you going to get a cup and get some – or are you going to bring buckets and fill them to capacity? That choice is yours!

Personal Standards - What are the standards that you set for yourself? Do you feel as if whatever the minimum is, that's good enough? If that's the way you feel, before long, the minimum required becomes the maximum effort you are willing to give! When I was in high school, I knew a guy named Dale. I knew Dale for three and a half years. On the very first day of class you could say, "Dale, how many?" and he would tell you how many days until summer vacation. That was all he was concerned with! I once had a class with Dale. He made a 75 on an exam, he turned around and look at me and said, "I guess I studied too hard for than one!" Dale's goal was just to get by with the least amount of effort. I have been to a few high school reunions since then and no one has ever heard of Dale since we graduated. If he's still alive, he's probably living under a bridge somewhere – just barely getting by. You should want to set high standards. It's better to aim for the stars and hit the moon; than aim for the moon and get stuck in the mud! Most people come to life with a teaspoon and say, "Give me my share." I say come to life with a bulldozer and get all you want – it's there, *all you have to do is go get it!*

When I got out of the Air Force in 1984, I had an electric powered dune buggy. I had been building full sized electric cars since I was a senior in high school. In fact, I actually built my first electric "car" when I was 10 years old and I removed the worn out gasoline engine from my go-cart and replaced it with a starter motor and a 12 volt car battery. Anyway, my dune buggy had a top speed of about 60 MPH and a range of about 50 or 60 miles per charge. When I went off the grid, I parked the car and used the batteries at my house, my Dad's A-Frame, and the well house that pumped our water.

It wasn't long after I hooked back up to the grid, that I began thinking about electric cars again and if I was going to build one today, how fast would it be and how far could I make it go. I set new goals. Top speed would be at least 75 miles per hour and the range would be 50 to 100 miles per charge. I began to think about how I could accomplish these ambitious goals. The car would have three wheels instead of four; so technically it would be classified as a motorcycle. Three wheels would reduce rolling resistance at slow speed and allow me to put an aerodynamic body on it to reduce drag at high speed.

This labor of love is a work in progress; however, I will say there is now a team working with me and we are in the testing stages with two prototypes being built. And as for achieving the goals I had set, in the very first road test operating on less than one third power, we hit a top speed of 41 miles per hour! We have no doubt that the maximum (ungoverned) speed will be over 100 miles per hour! With a full compliment of lead-acid batteries the range will be about 100 miles per day and with high performance lithium batteries, the range should be around 250 miles per charge. We anticipate starting custom production soon. You can follow our progress at www.ShockwaveMotors.com.

Dare to dream!

the Predator

Success Experiences – Quick wins build a positive mind set. The kinds of goals I have been talking about are long range goals, taking years to accomplish. You also want to set short term goals; goals that you can accomplish in a matter of days or weeks. When you first start setting goals, if you don't have some success experiences to look back on, it's very easy to get discouraged and just quit.

"I do not think there is any other quality so essential to success of any kind as the quality of perseverance. It overcomes almost everything, even nature."

J. D. Rockefeller

J. D. Rockefeller in 1885

Comparison With Others: Role Models – It's good to have people you look up to and respect. You should compare yourself with other people that you admire. Pick someone you think highly of, such as a hero, movie star, leader, family member, or friend. I don't mean you have to be like they are, but look at their behaviors, see what they have accomplished and how they did it!

Recognition and Rewards – The recognition and rewards we receive for our actions in life come from two sources: internal and external. We love it when someone comes up to us and tells us we did a great job. That pat on the back goes a long way. And certainly, we appreciate getting paid for the work we do. Those are examples of external rewards and recognition. But, what happens when no one is around, or they're to busy to tell us how we are doing? That's when the internal system kicks in into gear. Regrettably, our internal feedback is usually negative. It's ok to admit that we all talk to ourselves. (I usually don't worry until I notice someone is having a three or four way conversation with themselves – but that's another topic!) The point is most of what we tell ourselves all day long is negative.

We are constantly telling ourselves things like, no one cares about the job I do, it's all about production, my suggestions don't matter, I made a stupid mistake – and the list goes on. All day long we bombard ourselves with negativity and *if we can't believe ourselves, who can we believe?* So we believe the negative and our mind becomes numb by the constant reminder of how bad our life is, how stupid we are for making a dumb mistake, how miserable of a place this is to work, my supervisor ignores me, my spouse hates me, the kids are mean, the house is a wreck, etc. You get the picture, this destroys our positive attitude. It's up to us to turn this around. If your boss is too busy to notice your efforts, don't worry about it. You go ahead and walk away at the end of the day with your shoulders back and your head held high – telling yourself, "Yes, I did my very best today, I don't care who noticed or who didn't – *I noticed and I care!*"

Your attitude is truly your most important asset, protect it well. A positive attitude is not a guarantee of success. But a positive attitude will let you succeed at anything and everything better than a negative attitude will.

I invite you to visit the web site: www.4TrainingSolutions.info for more information on goal setting and self-motivation.

Photo courtesy
Paul J. Meyer

"Ninety percent of all those who fail in life are not actually defeated; they simply give up before achieving what they want. Often they do not even know what they want, why they want it, or how to get it."
Paul J. Meyer

Postscript: Today's Workforce

Any company (manufacturing or service) that makes an *extensive use* of "Temporary Agencies" and paying low wages to their employees is only fooling itself. Turnover rates of around 350% to 450% among temporary employees are not uncommon! Recruitment and training costs will run into the hundreds of thousands of dollars. Lost productivity is almost incalculable! Coupled with this, there is a growing tendency to hire Hispanic workers and it seems we are moving *away* from the high skills, highly trained workforce, back to the time when the assembly line was first put into use by Henry Ford. At that time, low skilled, low paid employees simply did exactly what they were told and attached that same part on the car for eight or more hours a day.

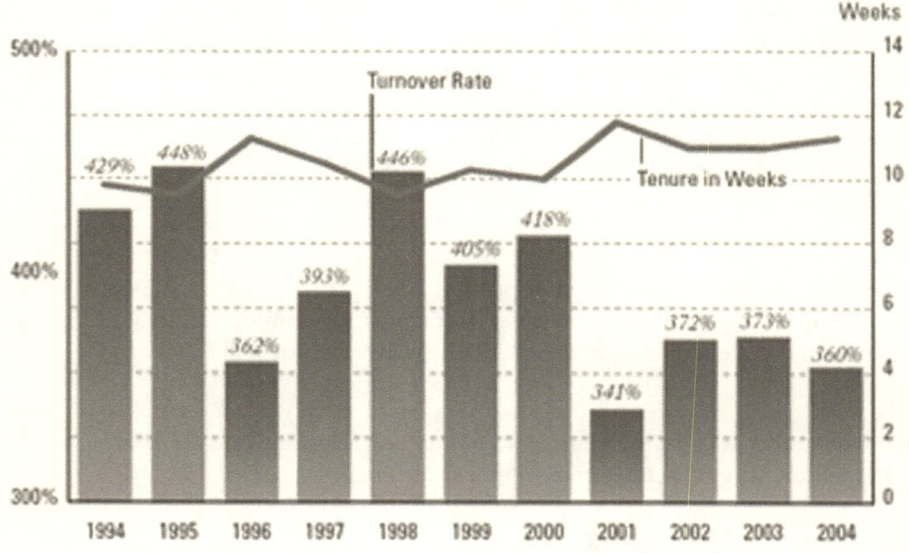

Source: American Staffing Association, Employment and Sales Survey

Figure 66 Temporary Employee Turnover Rates

Please don't misunderstand me, I am not running down the Hispanic worker. In fact, it has been my experience that the vast majority of Hispanic workers are highly motivated and extremely hard working! I have seen an Hispanic employee with a crippled leg work harder and faster than American employees! *However, three key points should be kept in mind: They must be legal; they must be educated; and they must have and use Basic English communication skills.* Not only is it hazardous and unsafe for the Hispanic employee to operate equipment when they can't read the operating instructions and precautions, it's dangerous for others working around them.

With a multilingual workforce we are faced with few choices. First, we could create all documents and training material in the English language and perhaps we would need to reduce everything to the lowest common denominator. We may be forced to use pictures and cartoons to illustrate how to do a job! The assembly lines of the 1920's were manned with European immigrates speaking little or no English. Their jobs were dull, boring, repetitive, low skilled, offering no chance of using imagination and creativity to improve the jobs. Are we moving back to that era? Our second choice is even more outlandish. Since some employees can not or *will not* speak English on the job, then *we could accommodate their needs!* I once worked with an American company located in the heart of North Carolina. They certainly had a large and diverse workforce. To accommodate the needs of the employees, they insisted that all material and training be presented in *five languages.* Every training program was created in English and then translated into Spanish, Korean, and two versions of Chinese!

It's been my experience that many of the Hispanic's know English; they just *refuse* to speak it. Personally, I believe we will build a stronger workplace if we institute English Only rules during working hours on the manufacturing floor. (Of course, people can speak any language they like on breaks.) Not only will this improve the safety of our work environment, but it will allow us to speak a common language. Without a common language, we can not communicate; no communication and the entire team building process crumbles like a house of cards.

I hate to be blunt, but an organization can not become a World Class Company by hiring people *(of any nationality – yes, even Americans)* if they are lacking in basic education and communication skills. What good does it do to give tests to gauge an applicant's reading, comprehension, and technical ability if you accept almost any score? *The bottom line is that companies will have to invest in their people and pay a competitive wage in order to attract and keep World Class People!*

Appendix:

VSM Symbols

The following list of common Value Stream Mapping Symbols and the Lean Manufacturing background information is courtesy of Strategos, Inc. for more information please visit www.strategosinc.com. Each organizations processes are unique, don't be afraid to experiment and create your own symbols!

VSM Process Symbols

Customer/Supplier	This icon represents the Supplier when in the upper left, the usual starting point for material flow. The customer is represented when placed in the upper right, the usual end point for material flow.
Process **Dedicated Process**	This icon is a process, operation, machine or department, through which material flows. Typically, to avoid unwieldy mapping of every single processing step, it represents one department with a continuous, internal fixed flow path. In the case of assembly with several connected workstations, even if some WIP inventory accumulates between machines (or stations), the entire line would show as a single box. If there are separate operations, where one is disconnected from the next, inventory between and batch transfers, then use multiple boxes.
Process **Shared Process**	This is a process operation, department or work center that other value stream families share. Estimate the number of operators required for the Value Stream being mapped, not the number of operators required for processing all products.
C/T= C/O= Batch= Avail= **Data Box**	This icon goes under other icons that have significant information/data required for analyzing and observing the system. Typical information placed in a Data Box underneath FACTORY icons is the frequency of shipping during any shift, material handling information, transfer batch size, demand quantity per period, etc. Typical information in a Data Box underneath MANUFACTURING PROCESS icons: · C/T (Cycle

	Time) - time (in seconds) that elapses between one part coming off the process to the next part coming off, · C/O (Changeover Time) - time to switch from producing one product on the process to another · Uptime- percentage time that the machine is available for processing · EPE (a measure of production rate/s) - Acronym stands for "Every Part Every___". · Number of operators - use OPERATOR icon inside process boxes · Number of product variations · Available Capacity · Scrap rate · Transfer batch size (based on process batch size and material transfer rate)
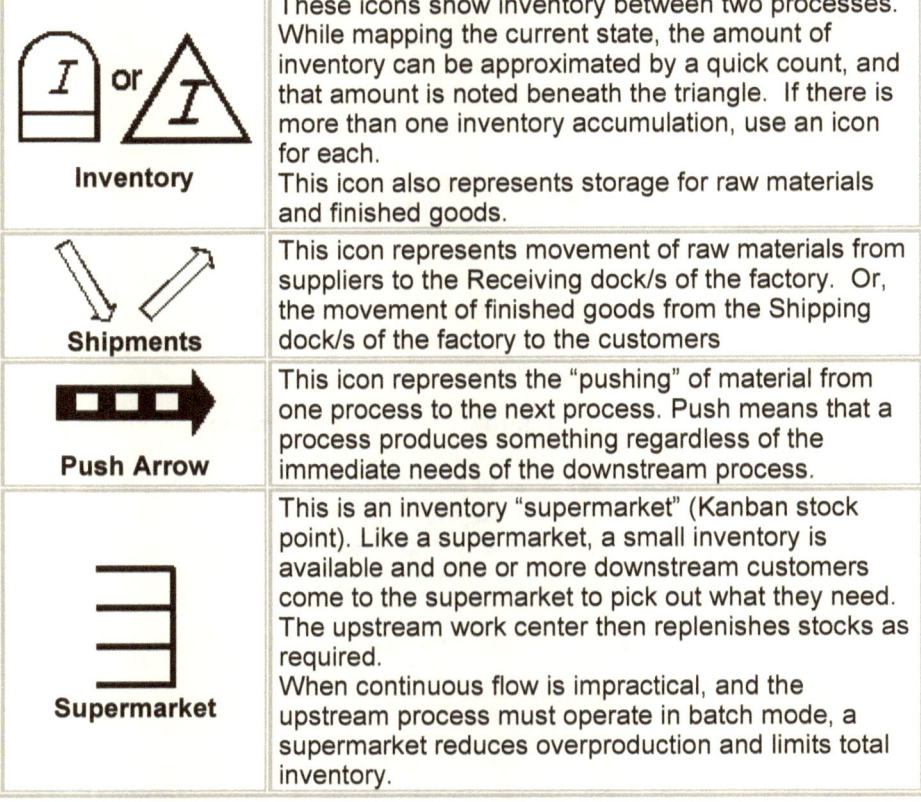 **Workcell**	This symbol indicates that multiple processes are integrated in a manufacturing workcell. Such cells usually process a limited family of similar products or a single product. Product moves from process step to process step in small batches or single pieces.

VSM Material Symbols

Inventory	These icons show inventory between two processes. While mapping the current state, the amount of inventory can be approximated by a quick count, and that amount is noted beneath the triangle. If there is more than one inventory accumulation, use an icon for each. This icon also represents storage for raw materials and finished goods.
Shipments	This icon represents movement of raw materials from suppliers to the Receiving dock/s of the factory. Or, the movement of finished goods from the Shipping dock/s of the factory to the customers
Push Arrow	This icon represents the "pushing" of material from one process to the next process. Push means that a process produces something regardless of the immediate needs of the downstream process.
Supermarket	This is an inventory "supermarket" (Kanban stock point). Like a supermarket, a small inventory is available and one or more downstream customers come to the supermarket to pick out what they need. The upstream work center then replenishes stocks as required. When continuous flow is impractical, and the upstream process must operate in batch mode, a supermarket reduces overproduction and limits total inventory.

Material Pull	Supermarkets connect to downstream processes with this "Pull" icon that indicates physical removal.
MAX=XX **FIFO Lane**	First-In-First-Out inventory. Use this icon when processes are connected with a FIFO system that limits input. An accumulating roller conveyor is an example. Record the maximum possible inventory.
Safety Stock	This icon represents an inventory "hedge" (or safety stock) against problems such as downtime, to protect the system against sudden fluctuations in customer orders or system failures. Notice that the icon is closed on all sides. It is intended as a temporary, not a permanent storage of stock; thus; there should be a clearly-stated management policy on when such inventory should be used.
External Shipment	Shipments from suppliers or to customers using external transport.

VSM Information Symbols

Production Control **Production Control**	This box represents a central production scheduling or control department, person or operation.
Daily **Manual Info**	A straight, thin arrow shows general flow of information from memos, reports, or conversation. Frequency and other notes may be relevant.
Monthly **Electronic Info**	This wiggle arrow represents electronic flow such as electronic data interchange (EDI), the Internet, Intranets, LANs (local area network), WANs (wide area network). You may indicate the frequency of information/data interchange, the type of media used ex. fax, phone, etc. and the type of data exchanged.
P **Production Kanban**	This icon triggers production of a pre-defined number of parts. It signals a supplying process to provide parts to a downstream process.
W	This icon represents a card or device that instructs a material handler to transfer parts from a supermarket to the receiving process. The material handler (or

Withdrawal Kanban	operator) goes to the supermarket and withdraws the necessary items.
Signal Kanban	This icon is used whenever the on-hand inventory levels in the supermarket between two processes drops to a trigger or minimum point. When a Triangle Kanban arrives at a supplying process, it signals a changeover and production of a predetermined batch size of the part noted on the Kanban. It is also referred as "one-per-batch" Kanban.
Kanban Post	A location where Kanban signals reside for pickup. Often used with two-card systems to exchange withdrawal and production Kanban.
Sequenced Pull	This icon represents a pull system that gives instruction to subassembly processes to produce a predetermined type and quantity of product, typically one unit, without using a supermarket.
Load Leveling	This icon is a tool to batch Kanbans in order to level the production volume and mix over a period of time
MRP/ERP	Scheduling using MRP/ERP or other centralized systems.
Go See	Gathering of information through visual means.
Verbal Information	This icon represents verbal or personal information flow.

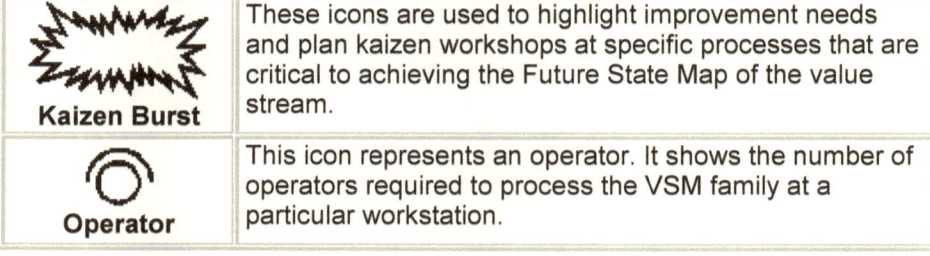

VSM General Symbols

Kaizen Burst	These icons are used to highlight improvement needs and plan kaizen workshops at specific processes that are critical to achieving the Future State Map of the value stream.
Operator	This icon represents an operator. It shows the number of operators required to process the VSM family at a particular workstation.

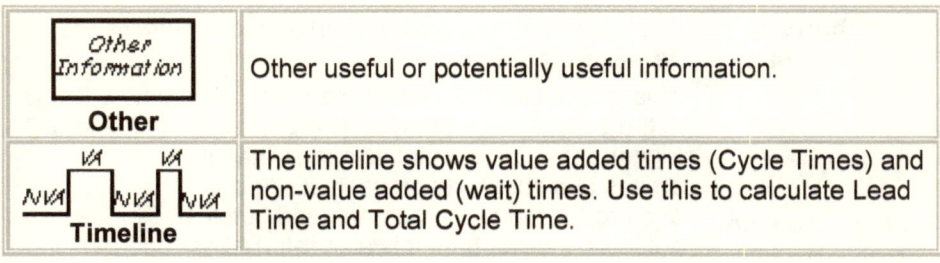**Other**	Other useful or potentially useful information.
Timeline	The timeline shows value added times (Cycle Times) and non-value added (wait) times. Use this to calculate Lead Time and Total Cycle Time.

Glossary of Terms

5 Why's - An effective method of analyzing and solving problems by asking "why?" five times (or as many times as needed to find the root cause).

5S - The principle of waste elimination through workplace organization. This is derived from the Japanese words Seiri, Seiton, Seiso, Seiketsu, and Shitsuke. In English the 5S are sort, straighten (or set in order), shine, standardize, and sustain.

7 Wastes - There are 7 types of waste that describe all wasteful activity in a production environment. Elimination of the 7 wastes leads to improved profits. The 7 wastes are 1) Overproduction, 2) Transportation, 3) Motion, 4) Waiting, 5) Processing, 6) Inventory, and 7) Defects.

A3 Report - This "A3" sized (11 inches x 17 inches) form is used at Toyota as a one-sheet problem evaluation, root cause analysis, and corrective action planning tool.

Andon - This is a tool of visual management, originating from the Japanese word for 'lamp'. Most commonly, andons are lights placed on machines or on production lines to indicate operation status.

Affinity Diagram - A tool used to organize ideas, usually generated through brainstorming, into groups of related thoughts. The emphasis is on a pre-rational, gut-fell sort of grouping, often done by the members of the group with little or no talking. The Affinity Diagram is also known as the KJ method after its creator, Kawakita Jiro.

Attributes Data - Data that is counted in discrete units such as dollars, hours, items, and yes/no options. The alternative to attributes data is variables data, which is data that is measured on a continuous and infinite scale such as temperature or distance. Charts that use attribute data include bar charts, pie charts, Pareto charts and some control charts.

Availability - A product or service's ability to perform its intended function at a given time and under appropriate conditions. It can be expressed by the ratio operative time/total time where operative time is the time that it is functioning or ready to function.

Average Chart (X-bar Chart) - A control chart in which the average of the subgroup, represented by the X-bar, is to determine the stability or lack thereof in the process. Average charts are usually paired with range charts or sample standard deviation charts for complete analysis.

Bar chart – This is a chart that compares different groups of data to each other through the use of bars that represent each group. Bar charts can be simple, in which each group of data consists of a single type of data, or grouped or stacked, in which the groups of data are broken down into internal categories.

Benchmarking - A technique that involves comparing one's own processes to excellent examples of similar processes in other organizations or departments. Through benchmarking, rapid learning can occur, and processes can undergo dramatic improvements.

Brainstorming - A tool used to encourage creative thinking and new ideas. A group formulates and records as many ideas as possible concerning a certain subject, regardless of the content of the ideas. No discussion, evaluation, or criticism of ideas is allowed until the brainstorming session is complete.

Breakthrough Thinking - This is a management technique which emphasizes the development of new, radical approaches to traditional constraints, as opposed to incremental or minor changes in thought that build on the original approach.

Business Process Redesign or Reengineering - A management method which stresses the fundamental rethinking of processes, questioning all assumptions, in an effort to streamline organizations and to focus on adding value in core processes.

Cause and Effect Diagram - A tool used to analyze all factors (causes) that contribute to a given situation or occurrence (effect) by breaking down main causes into smaller and smaller sub-causes. It is also known as the Ishikawa or the fishbone diagram.

Cellular Manufacturing – This is the layout of machines of different types performing different operations in a tight sequence, typically in a U-shape, to permit single piece flow and flexible deployment of human effort.

Chaku-Chaku- This is a method of conducting single-piece flow, where the operator proceeds from machine to machine, taking the part from one machine and loading it into the next.

Change Agent - The catalytic force moving firms and value streams out of the world of inward-looking batch-and-queue.

Change Management - The process of planning, preparing, educating, resource allocating, and implementing of a cultural change in an organization.

Changeover - The time from when the last good piece comes off of a machine or process until the first good piece of the next product is made.

Check Sheet - A customized form used to record data. Usually, it is used to record how often some activity occurs.

Checklist - A list of important steps that must take place in a process or any other activity.

Common causes - Inherent causes of variation in a process. They are typical of the process, not unexpected. That is not to say that they must be tolerated; on the contrary, once special causes of variation are largely removed, a focus on removing common causes of variation can pay big dividends.

Conformance to Requirements - Meeting requirements or specifications.

Continuous Improvement - On-going improvement of any and all aspects of an organization including products, services, communications, environment, functions, individual processes, etc. Also know as Kaizen.

Control Chart - A chart that indicates upper and lower statistical control limits, and an average line, for samples or subgroups of a given process. If all points on the control chart are within the limits, variation may be ascribed to common causes and the process is deemed to be "in control." If points fall outside the limits, it is an indication that special causes of variation are occurring, and the process is said to be "out of control."

Control Limit - A statistically-determined line on a control chart used to analyze variation within a process. If variation exceeds the control limits, then the process is being affected by special causes and is said to be "out of control." A control limit is not the same as a specification limit.

Cost of Poor Quality - The costs incurred by producing products or services of poor quality. These costs usually include the cost of inspection, rework, duplicate work, scrapping rejects, replacements and refunds, complaints, and loss of customers and reputation. "Cost of Quality" was Philip Crosby's term for the cost of poor quality.

Cp - Commonly used process capability index defined as [USL (upper spec limit) − LSL (lower spec limit)] / [6 x sigma], where sigma is the estimated process standard deviation.

Cpk - Commonly used process capability index defined as the lesser of USL - m / 3 sigma or m - LSL / 3 sigma, where sigma is the estimated process standard deviation.

Crosby, Philip - One of the quality guru's. Crosby founded several consulting agencies including Career IV, Philip Crosby Associates, and the Quality College. He has authored several books including Quality Is Free and Quality Without Tears. Crosby is well-known for his theory of "zero defects."

Current State Map - Helps visualize the current production process and identify sources of waste.

Customer - Any recipient of a product or service; anyone who is affected by what one produces. A customer can be external or outside the organization or they can be internal to the organization.

Cycle Time - The time required to complete one cycle of an operation. If cycle time for every operation in a complete process can be reduced to equal Takt time, products can be made in single-piece flow.

Defect -An error in construction of a product or service that renders it unusable; an error that causes a product or service to not meet requirements.

Deming Cycle - Alternate name for the Plan-Do-Check-Act cycle, a four-stage approach to problem-solving. It is also sometimes called the Shewhart cycle.

Deming, W. Edwards - Known as the father of quality control. Deming began his work in quality control in the United States in the 1930's. During World War II worked to aid the war effort. After the war, he went to Japan to help in the rebuilding of their country. His methods of quality control became an integral part of Japanese industry. Deming is a celebrated author and is well-known for his "14 Points" for effective management.

Design for Manufacturing (DFM) - Design for Manufacturing is an approach to design that fosters simultaneous involvement of product design, process design, and manufacturing.

Design of Experiments (DOE) - Planning and conducting experiments and evaluating the results. The outcome of a design of experiment includes a mathematical equation predicting the interaction of the factors influencing a process and the relevant output characteristics of the process.

Employee Involvement (Quality Circles/Quality Teams) – This is the regular participation of employees in decision-making and suggestions. The driving forces behind increasing the involvement of employees are the conviction that more brains are better, that people in the process know it best, and that involved employees will be more motivated to do what is best for the organization.

Empowerment - Usually refers to giving employees decision-making and problem-solving authority within their jobs.

Error Proofing - A process used to prevent errors from occurring or to immediately point out a defect as it occurs. This is also known as "Poka-Yoke."

External customer - A person or organization outside your organization who receives the output of a process. Of all external customers, the end-user should be the most important.

Failure Mode Effects Analysis (FMEA) - A technique that systematically analyzes the types of failures which will be expected as a product is used, and what the effects of each "failure mode" will be.

Facilitator - Person who helps a team with issues of teamwork, communication, and problem-solving. A facilitator should not contribute to the actual content of the team's project, focusing instead as an observer of the team's functioning as a group.

Fishbone Diagram - Another name for a cause & effect diagram, derived from the original shape of the diagram as used by its creator, Kaoru Ishikawa.

Flowchart - A graphical representation of a given process delineating each step. It is used to diagram how the process actually functions and where waste, error, and frustration enter the process.

Force Field Analysis - A tool, developed by social psychologist Kurt Lewin, which is used to analyze the opposing forces involved in causing/resisting any change. It is shown in balance sheet format with forces that will help (driving forces) listed on the left and forces that hinder (restraining forces) listed on the right.

Frequency Distribution - An organization of data, usually in a chart, which depicts how often a different event occurs. A histogram is one common type of frequency distribution, and a frequency polygon is another.

Gantt chart - A bar chart that shows planned work and finished work in relation to time. Each task in a list has a bar corresponding to it. The length of the bar is used to indicate the expected or actual duration of the task.

Gemba - This is a Japanese word meaning "actual place," or the place where you work to create value.

Gembutsu - Japanese for 'actual thing' or 'actual product'.

Genjitsu - Japanese for 'the facts' or 'the reality'.

Hanedashi - Auto-eject devices that unload the part from the machine once the cycle is complete.

Heijunka - A method of leveling production at the final assembly line that makes just-in-time production possible.

Histogram - This is a problem solving tool that displays data graphically in distribution.

Hoshin Kanri - Japanese term for hoshin planning, a form of interactive, strategic, planning which aids the flow of information up and down the organizational layers in a systematic, productive way.

Hoshin Planning - A method of strategic planning for quality. It helps executives integrate quality improvement into the organization's long-range plan. According to the GOAL/QPC Health Care Application Research Committee, "Hoshin Planning is a method used to ensure that the mission, vision, goals, and annual objectives of an organization are communicated to and implemented by everyone, from the executive level to the 'front line' level."

Indicator - Quantitative measure of performance. Indicators are usually ratios comparing the number of occurrences a certain phenomenon and the number of times the phenomenon could have occurred.

Internal Customer – Typically this person is the next step in the process, someone within your organization, further downstream in a process, who receives the output of your work.

Ishikawa Diagram - Another name for the cause & effect diagram, after its inventor, Kaoru Ishikawa.

Ishikawa, Kaoru - One of Japan's quality control pioneers. He developed the cause & effect diagram (Ishikawa diagram) in 1943 and published many books addressing quality control. In addition to his work at Kawasaki, Ishikawa was a long-standing member of the Union of Japanese Scientists and Engineers and an assistant professor at the University of Tokyo.

Juran, Joseph M. - One of the great quality gurus, and, like Deming, an early student of the work of Walter Shewhart at Western Electric. His work has specialized in linking management to quality engineering. Dr. Juran is the founder of the Juran Institute which has long been the vehicle of his work in quality management and is well-known for espousing "the quality trilogy" of quality planning, quality control, and quality improvement. Juran has authored many books and other works in an effort to spread awareness of quality management ideas and applications.

Jidoka - This is stopping a line automatically when a defective part is detected.

Jishu Kanri - Self

Judgment Inspection - A form of inspection used to determine non-conforming product.

Just-in-Time (JIT) - Making what the customer needs when the customer needs it in the quantity the customer needs, using minimal resources of manpower, material, and machinery.

Jutsu - This means to talk, or 'the art of' (i.e., 'leanjutsu: the art of lean production').

Kai-aku - This is the opposite of kaizen. Change for the worse.

Kaikaku - This is radical improvements or reform that affects the future value stream.

Kaizen - A Japanese word meaning continuous improvement through constant striving to reach higher standards.

Kaizen Blitz - A fast and focused process for improving some component of business a product line, a machine, or a process. It utilizes a cross-functional team of employees for a quick problem-solving exercise, where they focus on designing solutions to meet some well-defined goals.

Kaizen Event - Any action whose output is intended to be an improvement to an existing process.

Kaizen Newspaper - A tool for visually managing continuous improvement suggestions.

Kanban - This is a Japanese term which means card signal (Signboard). Kanban is the information signal used to indicate the need for material replenishment in a pull production process.

Kano Methods - This a model using three types of product requirements which influence customer satisfaction in different ways.

Karoshi - Death from overwork.

KJ method - Another name for the affinity diagram, after its inventor, Kawakita Jiro.

Lead Time - The total time a customer must wait to receive a product after placing an order.

Lean - A business practice characterized by the endless pursuit of waste elimination.

Lean Transformation - Developing a culture that is intolerant to waste in all of its forms.

Leveling - Smoothing out the production schedule by averaging out both the volume and mix of products.

Line Balancing - This in the process of evenly distributing both the quantity and variety of work across available work time, avoiding overburden and under use of resources. This eliminates bottlenecks and downtime, which translates into shorter flow time.

Machine Cycle Time - The time it takes for a machine to produce one unit.

Machine Work - This is work that is done by a machine.

Manual Work - This is the work that is done by people.

Mean -The average of a group of measurement values. Mean is determined by dividing the sum of the values by the number of values in the group.

Median - The middle of a group of measurement values when arranged in numerical order. For example, in the group (32, 45, 78, 79, 101), 78 is the median. If the group contains an even number of values, the median is the average of the two middle values.

Mission Statement - This is a written declaration of the purpose of an organization or project team. Organizational mission or vision statements often include an organizational vision for the future, goals, and values.

Mode - The most frequently occurring value in a large group of measurements.

Multi-Tasking - Breaking into one activity before it is complete to move onto at least one other task before returning complete the original task.

Mura - This is variations and variability in work method or the output of a process.

Muri - This means exertion, overworking (a person or machine), and unreasonableness.

Nagara - Accomplishing more than one task in one motion or function. This is Japanese for 'while doing something'.

Nominal Group Technique - Technique used to encourage creative thinking and new ideas, but is more controlled than brainstorming. Each member of a group writes down his or her ideas and then contributes one to the group pool. All contributed ideas are then discussed and prioritized.

np Chart - A control chart indicating the number of defective units in a given sample.

Paradigm - A way of thinking about a given subject that defines how one views events, relationships, ideas, etc. within the boundaries of that subject.

One Piece Flow - Producing one unit at a time, as opposed to producing in large lots. (From Advanced Manufacturing)

One-Touch Exchange of Dies (OTED) - The reduction of die set-up where die setting is reduced to a single step.

Open Room Effect - This common practice in Japanese offices involves taking down the walls and cubicles of an office and laying all of the desks out into one big 'open room'.

Operator Cycle Time - The time it takes for a worker or machine operator to complete a sequence of operations, including loading and unloading, but not including waiting time.

Overall Equipment Effectiveness (OEE) - Calculated as Availability x Performance x Quality to determine how much of the time a piece of equipment is being used while it is actually making good parts at an appropriate speed.

Overproduction - Producing more, sooner or faster than is required by the next process or customer.

Pacemaker - A device or technique use to set the pace of production and maintain Takt time.

Pareto Chart - A bar chart that orders data from the most frequent to the least frequent, allowing the analyst to determine the most important factor in a given situation or process.

Pareto Principle - The idea here is that a few root problems are responsible for the large majority of consequences. The Pareto principle is derived from the work of Vilfredo Pareto, a turn-of-the-century Italian economist who studied the distributions of wealth in different countries. He concluded that a fairly consistent minority; about 20%; of people controlled the large majority; about 80%; of a society's wealth. This same distribution has been observed in other areas and has been termed the Pareto principle. It is defined by J. M. Juran as the idea that 80% of all effects are produced by only 20% of the possible causes.

Percent Chart (p Chart) - A control chart that determines the stability of a process by finding what percentage of total units in a sample are defective.

Pie Chart - A chart compares groups of data to the whole data set by showing each group as a "slice" of the entire "pie." Pie charts are particularly useful for investigating what percentage each group represents.

Plan-Do-Check-Act (PDCA) Cycle - A four-step improvement process originally conceived of by Walter A. Shewhart. The first step involves planning for the necessary improvement; the second step is the implementation of the plan; the third step is to check the results of the plan; the last step is to act upon the results of the plan. It is also known as the Shewhart cycle, the Deming cycle, and the PDCA cycle.

Poka-Yoke - Japanese word that refers to a mistake-proofing device or procedure used to prevent a defect during the production process.

Policy Deployment – This is another name for hoshin planning.

Population - Total set of items from which a sample set is taken.

Process Capability - 1. A statistical measure indicating the inherent variation for a given event in a stable process, usually defined as the process width divided by 6 sigma. 2. Competence of the process, based on tested performance, to achieve certain results.

Process Capability Index - Measurement indicating the ability of a process to produce specified results. Cp and Cpk are two process capability indices.

Quality Assurance (QA) - Generally refers to the post-production checks, inspection, or reviews done to ensure quality of a product or service.

Quality Audit - An independent investigation and assessment of quality activities and results to determine whether or not the quality plan is effective and appropriate.

Quality Circles - 1. Quality improvement teams or groups. 2. In Japan, groups of employees formed for the study of and sharing information regarding quality control issues and theory.

Quality Control – This is the use of techniques and activities that compare actual quality performance with goals and define appropriate action in response to a shortfall.

Quality Improvement - A systematic approach to the processes of work that looks to remove waste, loss, rework, frustration, etc. in order to make the processes of work more effective, efficient, and appropriate.

Quality Improvement Team - This is a group of employees that take on a project to improve a given process or design a new process within an organization.

Quality Function Deployment (QFD) - A technique used to translate customer requirements into appropriate goals for each stage of product or service development and output. The two approaches to quality function deployment are known as the House of Quality and the Matrix of Matrices.

Quality Loss Function - This is an algebraic function that illustrates the loss of quality that occurs when a characteristic deviates from its target value. It is expressed often in monetary terms. Dr. Genichi Taguchi coined this term; his work suggests that quality losses vary as the square of the deviation from target.

Range Chart - Control chart in which the range of the subgroup is used to track the instantaneous variation within a process, i.e. the variation in the process at any one time, when many input factors would not have time to vary enough to make a detectable difference. Range charts are usually paired with average charts for complete analysis.

Recorder - This is the team member that takes minutes during team meetings to capture team's progress. Once the team is well underway, this role can be rotated through out the group.

Regression Analysis - A statistical technique used to determine the best mathematical expression to describe the relationship between a response and independent variables.

Reliability - The probability of a product or service successfully doing its job under given conditions.

Robust - This is the ability of a product or service to function appropriately regardless of external conditions and other uncontrollable factors.

Robust Design – This is an approach to the planning of new products and services that harnesses Taguchi methods.

Root Cause - The most basic underlying reason for an event or condition.

Run Chart - This is also known as a line chart, or line graph. It is a chart that plots data over time, allowing you to identify trends and anomalies.

Sample - A subset of a population used to represent the population in statistical analysis. Samples are almost always random, which means that all individuals in the population are equally likely to be chosen for the sample.

Sample Standard Deviation Chart (s chart) - Control chart in which the standard deviation of the subgroup is tracked to determine the variation within a process over time. Sample standard deviation charts are usually paired with average charts for complete analysis.

Scatter Diagram (Scatter Plot) - A tool that studies the possible relationship between two variables expressed on the x-axis and y-axis of a graph. The direction and density of the points plotted will indicate various relationships or a lack of any relationship between the variables.

Seven Tools of Quality - Quality improvement tools that include the histogram, Pareto chart, check sheet, control chart, cause-and-effect diagram, flowchart, and scatter diagram.

Seven Wastes - Taiichi Ohno's original catalog of the wastes commonly found in physical production. These are overproduction ahead of demand, waiting for the next processing stop, unnecessary transport of materials, over-processing of parts due to poor tool and product design, inventories more than the absolute minimum, unnecessary movement by employees during the course of their work, and production of defective parts.

Shewhart Cycle - This is another name for the Plan-Do-Check-Act cycle. It is also sometimes called the Deming cycle.

Shewhart, Walter A. - He is known as the father of statistical process control or statistical quality control. He pioneered statistical quality control and improvement methods when he worked for Western Electric and Bell Telephone in the early decades of the 20th century.

Single Minute Exchange of Dies (SMED) - A series of techniques designed for changeovers of production machinery in less than ten minutes.

Single-Piece Flow - A process in which products proceed, one complete product at a time, through various operations in design, order-taking and production without interruptions, backflows or scrap.

Six Sigma - A methodology and set of tools used to improve quality to than 3.4 defects per million defect opportunities or better.

Special Causes - Causes of variation in a process that are not inherent in the process itself but originate from circumstances that are out of the ordinary. Special causes are indicated by points that fall outside the limits of a control chart.

Specification Limit - An engineering or design requirement that must be met in order to produce a product that meets our quality standard.

Statistical Process Control (SPC) and Statistical Quality control (SQC) - Analysis and control of a process through the use of statistical techniques; particularly control charts.

Structural Variation - Variation caused by recurring system-wide changes such as seasonal changes or long-term trends.

Supermarket - A tool of the pull system that helps signal demand for the product. In a supermarket, a fixed amount of raw material, work in process, or finished material is kept as a buffer to schedule variability or an incapable process.

Supplier - This is anyone whose output (materials, information, service, etc.) becomes an input to another person or group in a process of work. A supplier can be external or internal to the organization.

Taguchi, Genichi - He developed a set of practices known as Taguchi Methods, as they are known in the U.S., for improving quality while reducing costs. Taguchi Methods focus on the design of efficient experiments, and the increasing of signal to noise ratios. Dr. Taguchi also articulated the developed the quality loss function. Currently, he is executive director of the American Supplier Institute and director of the Japan Industrial Technology Institute.

Takt Time - Daily production number required to meet orders in hand divided into the number of working hours in the day. It is the heartbeat of the production system.

Tampering (Tweaking) - Dr. Deming cautions against tampering with systems that are "in control." It is very common for management to react to variation which is in fact normal, thereby starting wild goose chases after sources of problems which don't exist. Tampering with stable processes actually increases variation.

Tree Diagram - A chart used to break any task, goal, or category into increasingly detailed levels of information. Family trees are the classic example of a tree diagram.

Timekeeper - Team member who keeps track of time spent on each agenda item during team meetings. This job can easily be rotated among team members.

Total Productive Maintenance (TPM) - Maximizing equipment effectiveness and uptime throughout the entire life of the equipment.

Total Quality Leadership (TQL) and Total Quality Management (TQM) - This is managing for quality in all aspects of an organization focusing on employee participation and customer satisfaction. Often used as a catch-all phrase for implementing various quality control and improvement tools.

Toyota Production System (TPS) - This is a methodology that resulted from over 50 years of Kaizen at Toyota. TPS is built on a foundation of Leveling, with the supporting pillars of Just-in-Time and Jidoka. Parts of the TPS has is roots in the Deming's 14 Points.

Type I Error - Rejecting something that is acceptable. This is also known as an alpha error.

Type II Error - Accepting something that should have been rejected. This is also known as beta error.

u Chart - A control chart showing the count of defects per unit in a series of random samples.

Value Stream - A value stream is a series of all actions required to fulfill a customer's request, both value added and not.

Value stream mapping - This is the process of directly observing the flows of information and materials as they now occur, summarizing them visually, and then envisioning a future state with much better performance.

Value-Added Work - Work accomplished that the customer is willing to pay for. This is a transformation of the shape or function of the material/information in a way that the customer will pay for.

Variables Data - This is data that is measured on a continuous and infinite scale such as temperature, distance, and pressure rather than in discreet units or yes/no options. Variables data is used to create histograms, some control charts, and sometimes run charts.

Variance - This is a measure of deviation from the mean in a sample or population.

Variation - Change in the output or result of a process. Variation can be caused by common causes, special causes, tampering, or structural variation.

Vision - Often incorporated into an organizational mission (or vision) statement to clarify what the organization hopes to be doing at some point in the future. The vision should act as a guide in choosing courses of action for the organization.

Visual Control - The placement in plain view of all tools, parts, production activities, and indicators of production system performance so everyone involved can understand the status of the system at a glance.

Visual Management - Simple visual tools are used to identify the target state, and any deviance is met with corrective action.

Waste - Anything that uses resources, but does not add real value to the product or service.

Water Spider - This is a skilled and well-trained person who makes the rounds supplying parts, assisting with changeover, providing tools and materials.

Work Cell - A logical and productive grouping of machinery, tooling, and people which produces a family of similar products.

Work in Process (WIP) - Product or inventory in various stages of completion throughout the plant, from raw material to completed product.

Work Sequence - The defined steps and activities that need to be performed in order for the work to be completed.

Zero Defects - Philip Crosby's recommended performance standard that leaves no doubt regarding the goal of total quality. Crosby's theory holds that people can continually move closer to this goal by committing themselves to their work and the improvement process.

Bibliography

American Staffing Association, May-Jun 2005, *Staffing Success.*

Basic Improvement Tools. Madison, WI: Joiner Associates. a. Instructor Guide, p. 13. b. Workbook, p. 60.

Brassard, M., & Ritter, D. (1994). *The memory jogger II: A pocket guide of tools for continuous improvement and effective planning.* Methuen, MA: GOAL/QPC.

Commandant's planning guidance (July 1, 1995). Washington, DC: Headquarters of the U.S. Marine Corps.

De Bono, Edward (1967). *The Use of Lateral Thinking,* Jonathan Cape, London

Deming, W. E. (1986). *Out of the Crisis.* Cambridge, MA: Massachusetts Institute of Technology, Center for Advanced Engineering Study.

Deming, W. E. (1993). *The new economics for industry, government, education.* Cambridge, MA: Massachusetts Institute of Technology, Center for Advanced Engineering Study.

Deming, W.E. Seminar on Quality, Productivity, and Competitive Position, Student Notebook, p. 47. Wailea, Maui, HI, 12-15 JAN 1993. Los Angeles, CA: Quality Enhancement Seminars, Inc.

Department of the Navy (November 1992). *Fundamentals of Total Quality Leadership* (Instructor Guide), pp, 6-30 - 6-34. San Diego, CA: Navy Personnel Research and Development Center.

Department of the Navy. (March 1994). *Department of the Navy Total Quality Leadership Glossary* (TQLO Pub. No. 94-01). Washington, DC: Total Quality Leadership Office, Department of the Navy.

Department of the Navy. (September 7, 1994). *From the sea: Preparing the naval service for the 21st Century.* Washington, DC: Author.

Department of the Navy (November 1992). *Introduction to Total Quality Leadership,* pp. 6-18 - 6-19. Pensacola, FL: NET Program Management Support Activity.

Department of the Navy (September 1993). *Systems Approach to Process Improvement* (Instructor Guide), Lesson 2. San Diego, CA: OUSN Total Quality Leadership Office and Navy Personnel Research and Development Center

Dobyns, L., & Crawford-Mason, C. (1994). *Thinking about quality.* New York: Random House Times Books.

Dockstader, S. L. (1984). What to do when there are more than five deadly diseases. Presentation to the *MIT Conference on Quality and Productivity,* San Diego, CA.

Doherty, L. M. (May 1990). Managing the transformation: A two-phase approach to implementing TQM. Presentation at the *Third Annual Federal Quality and Productivity Conference*, Vienna, VA.

Doherty, L. M., & Howard, J. D. (January-February 1994). Total quality leadership above and below the waves. *Journal for Quality and Participation, 74*(1), 46-53.

Ford, Henry (1922), *My Life and Work*, Nevins and Hill

Ford Motor Company (July 1983). Continuing Process Control and Process Capability Improvement, Statistical Methods Office, Operations Support Staffs, Ford Motor Company

Gitlow, H., Gitlow, S., Oppenheim, A., Oppenheim, R. (1989). *Tools and Methods for the Improvement of Quality*. Homewood, IL: Richard D. Irwin, Inc.

Gluck, F. W., Kaufman, S., & Walleck, A. S. (1982). Four phases of strategic management. *Journal of Business Strategy, 2*(3), 9-21.

Goodstein, L. D., Nolan, T. M., & Pfeiffer, J. W. (1992). *Applied strategic planning: A comprehensive guide*. San Diego, CA: Pfeiffer & Co.

Gore, A. (September 7, 1993). *From red tape to results: Creating a government that works better & costs less* (Report of the National Performance Review). Washington , DC: Government Printing Office.

Government Performance and Results Act of 1993 (Public Law 103-62). (August 3, 1993). Washington, DC: U.S. Congress.

Houston, A., & Dockstader, S. L. (1993). *A Total Quality Leadership process improvement model* (TQLO Pub. No. 93-02). Washington, DC: Total Quality Leadership Office, Department of the Navy.

Houston, A & Dockstader, S. L. (1997). *Total Quality Leadership: A Primer* (TQLO Publ. No. 97-02). Washington DC: Department of the Navy Total Quality Leadership Office

Houston, A., Sheposh, J., & Shettel-Neuber, J. (1986). *Management methods for quality improvement based on statistical process control: A literature and field survey* (NPRDC Tech. Rep. 86-21). San Diego, CA: Navy Personnel Research and Development Center.

Ivancevich, J. M., Lorenzi, P., Skinner, S. J., & Crosby, P. B. (1994). *Management: Quality and competitiveness*. Boston: Irwin.

Kotter, J. (March-April 1995). Leading change: Why transformation efforts fail. *Harvard Business Review, 73*(2), 59-67.

Kumar, Sandeep, *Sandeep's Quality Page*, Delhi- India, http://members.rediff.com/quality/qualglos.htm

Ledford, G. E., Lawler, E. E., & Mohrman, S. A. (1990). The quality circle and its variations. In Campbell and Associates (Eds.), *Productivity in organizations*. San Francisco: Jossey-Bass.

Maslow, A. *A Theory of Human Motivation*, Psychological Review 50 (1943):370-96.

Maslow, A. (1954). *Motivation and Personality*, New York: Harper.

Meyer, Paul J., (1983) *The Dynamics of Goal Setting*, Success Motivation Institute

Metz, E. (Summer 1984). Managing change: Implementing productivity and quality improvements. *National Productivity Review, 3*(3), 303-314.

Ohno, T. (1988*). Toyota Production System: Beyond Large-Scale Production*, Productivity Press

Ohno, T. (1988). *Workplace Management*, Productivity Press

Ohno, T. (2007). *Taiichi Ohno's Workplace Management*, Translated by Jon Miller, Gemba Press

Roberts, Jack, *Total Productive Maintenance*. Department of Industrial and Engineering Technology; Texas A&M University-Commerce

Rodriguez, A., Landau, S., & Konoske, P. (1993). *Systems approach to process improvement* (Course No. CINP-500-0004). Washington, DC: Department of the Navy.

Rummler, G. A., & Brache, A. P. (January 1991). *Managing the white space. Training, 28*(1), 55-70.

Scherkenbach, W. W. (1988). *The Deming route to quality and productivity*. Rockville, MD: Mercury Press.

Scholtes, P. R., et. al. (1989). *The team handbook: How to use teams to improve quality*. Wisconsin: Joiner Associates.

Shewhart, W. (1939, in Deming, 1986). *Statistical method from the viewpoint of quality control.* New York: Dover.

Shingo, S. (1985*). A Revolution in Manufacturing: The SMED System*, Productivity Press

Shingo, S. (1989). A *Study of the Toyota Production System*, Productivity Press

Shingo, S. (1996). *Quick Changeover for Operators: The SMED System*, Productivity Press

Silberstang, J. (1995). *Charting the course: The Department of the Navy Total Quality Leadership curriculum guide* (TQLO Pub. No. 95-01). Washington, DC: Total Quality Leadership Office, Department of the Navy.

Strategos, Inc., www.strategosinc.com

Suarez, J. G. (1992). *Three experts on quality: Philip B. Crosby, W. Edwards Deming, J. M. Juran* (TQLO Pub. No. 92-02). Washington, DC: Total Quality Leadership Office, Department of the Navy.

Suarez, J. G. (1993). *Managing fear in the workplace* (TQLO Pub. No. 93-01). Washington, DC: Total Quality Leadership Office, Department of the Navy.

Superfactory, *Glossary*, www.superfactory.com

Tichy, N. (1983). *Managing strategic change.* New York: John Wiley. Howard, J. D. (1992). The only way ahead. *Naval Institute Proceedings, 118*(6), 85-86.

Tichy, N. M., & Devanna, M. A. (1990). *The transformational leader.* New York: John Wiley.

Tribus, M. (1988). *Quality first: Selected papers on quality and productivity improvement* (Pub. No. 1459). Washington, DC: National Society of Professional Engineers.

United States Air Force (August 1991). *The Metrics Handbook* (1st Ed.), p. A-25.

U.S. Air Force (Undated). *Process Improvement Guide - Total Quality Tools for Teams and Individuals*, pp. 61 - 81. Air Force Electronic Systems Center, Air Force Materiel Command.

Walton, M., (1990). *Deming management at work.* New York: Putnam.

Wasik, J., & Ryan, B. (1993). *TQL In the fleet: From theory to practice* (TQLO Pub. No. 93-05). Washington, DC: Total Quality Leadership Office, Department of the Navy.

Wells, D. L., (1996). *Strategic management for senior leaders: A handbook for implementation* (TQLO Pub. No. 96-03). Washington, DC: Total Quality Leadership Office, Department of the Navy.

Wells, D. L., & Doherty, L. M. (1994). *A handbook for strategic planning* (TQLO Pub. No. 94-02). Washington, DC: Total Quality Leadership Office, Department of the Navy.

Wheeler, D. J. (1993). *Understanding Variation - The Key to Managing Chaos.* Knoxville, TN: SPC Press.

Wheeler, D. J., & Chambers, D. S. (1992). *Understanding Statistical Process Control* (2nd Ed.). Knoxville, TN: SPC Press.

Wikipedia, http://en.wikipedia.org/

Womack, J. & Jones, D. (1990) *Lean Thinking.* Free Press

www.ingramcontent.com/pod-product-compliance
Lightning Source LLC
Chambersburg PA
CBHW032022170526
45157CB00002B/820